总顾问：牛　健　丁国声
总主编：任静生

职场综合英语教程
（第三册）

主　编：陈立伟
副主编：吴平安　张　蕾　龚　婷
编　者：王晓耘　梅　玲　刘　琳
　　　　赵　荃　栾　鸾　丁亚娟
　　　　陈颖宇

北京大学出版社
PEKING UNIVERSITY PRESS

图书在版编目(CIP)数据

职场综合英语教程.第3册/陈立伟主编.—北京：北京大学出版社，2014.2
（全国职业技能英语系列教材）

ISBN 978-7-301-23547-8

Ⅰ.①职… Ⅱ.①陈… Ⅲ.①英语—高等职业教育—教材 Ⅳ.①H31

中国版本图书馆CIP数据核字(2013)第290621号

书　　　　名：	职场综合英语教程（第三册）
著作责任者：	陈立伟　主编
策　　　　划：	谢尚楹　万晶晶
责 任 编 辑：	郝妮娜
标 准 书 号：	ISBN 978-7-301-23547-8/H·3436
出 版 发 行：	北京大学出版社
地　　　　址：	北京市海淀区成府路205号　100871
网　　　　址：	http://www.pup.cn　新浪官方微博：@北京大学出版社
电 子 信 箱：	zbing@pup.pku.edu.cn
电　　　　话：	邮购部 62752015　发行部 62750672　编辑部 62759634　出版部 62754962
印 　刷　 者：	北京大学印刷厂
经 　销 　者：	新华书店
	787毫米×1092毫米　16开本　8.25印张　260千字
	2014年2月第1版　2016年12月第4次印刷
定　　　　价：	38.00元（附光盘、教学电子课件）

未经许可，不得以任何方式复制或抄袭本书之部分或全部内容。
版权所有，侵权必究
举报电话：010-62752024　电子信箱：fd@pup.pku.edu.cn

前　言

职业化已经成为高职高专教育最显著的特征。增加实训、强调动手能力、采用"订单式"培养模式是其主要特色。在这种背景下，按照传统的教学方法进行基础课教学已经不容置疑地受到了挑战。就目前情况论，高职高专的基础课教学必须践行"以服务为宗旨，以就业为导向"的专业建设指导思想。在课程建设以及基础课教学内容中，必须结合学生的专业需求，有意识地融入与职场相关联的知识。

根据教育部《高职高专英语教育课程教学基本要求》的精神，联合国家级示范高职院校和骨干高职院校的一线教师，在充分调查现有高职高专英语教材的基础上，结合高职英语教学的未来发展趋势，在"安徽省高职高专外语教研会"的组织及北京大学出版社的支持下，编写了本套《职场综合英语教程》，并被列入普通高等教育"十二五"规划教材。

本套教程分为基础篇、第一册、第二册和第三册，共四册。

基础篇　主要针对英语基础比较薄弱的学生，融入了对音标的训练，旨在帮助这部分学生巩固英语的基础知识，为后续课程的学习奠定必要的基础。

第一册　主要涉及西方文化和日常生活，内容涵盖西方名人、青年旅馆、主题公园、肥皂剧、网上购物等。鲜活的内容、生活化的主题，有利于学生顺利融入大学生活，同时也有助于培养学生对英语学习的兴趣，为今后的职业化过渡打下坚实基础。

第二册　主要涉及求职以及职业素养培养等主题，如求职、自主创业、职场中人际交往和做好服务、科技与生活、名人的成功与失败等。另外，本册内容与职场文化的有机融合有利于学生对未来职业规划形成初步的认识。

第三册　从职场生活出发，针对高职学生可能遇到的职场活动进行设计，内容包括机场接待、银行服务、汽车制造等。内容难度适中，选材谨慎，真正做到通识化与职场化有机统筹，有助于学生以后进一步学习相关的专业英语。

本套教材的内容主要分为六个方面：听说、阅读、语法、应用文写作、文化速递与拓展词汇。

听说部分　践行任务型教学的指导思想，强调能听懂简单对话，能记录关键词，能就所给事物说出英语名称，或进行角色分工，完成简单对话。这部分设计了热身环节，通过比较容易完成的任务，帮助学生尽快进入相关主题的学习。而角色扮演部分则试

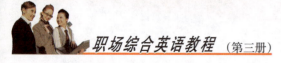

图充分调动学生的想象力和创造力,按照角色分工完成任务。听说部分还设计了听写内容,旨在培养学生听懂并记录关键词的能力。

阅读部分　由两篇相关主题的文章组成,其中第一篇为主要文章,教师应该进行精深讲解;第二篇属于附加文章,教师可以把它作为泛读教材使用。目的是让学生在阅读过程中完成对该主题的英语核心词汇的巩固和学习,同时深刻理解英语的语句结构。

语法部分　旨在夯实高职高专学生的语法基础,改善语法能力薄弱的现状,同时结合"高等学校英语应用能力考试"要求,对一些考试技巧进行精解,真正做到融会贯通,为提高英语综合能力打下良好基础。

写作部分　紧扣职场,重在应用文的写作。提供较规范的写作模式与常用句型供学生参考,通过实际的操练让学生进一步熟悉并掌握多种应用文的写作。

文化速递　是本套教材的特色之一。是针对单元主题的拓展性学习资料,可以帮助学生开阔视野、拓展知识面,提高综合人文素养。

词汇部分　依据大纲要求,课文中涉及的生词均分级标出。标★为A级词汇,标☆为超纲词汇。方便教师把握教学重点,也方便学生分级掌握词汇,逐步进级。

本套教材配有教学课件。每个单元针对不同的主题都有话题的进一步延伸,有利于教师进行拓展教学。丰富授课内容,活跃课堂气氛,激发学生的学习兴趣。

本套教材得到教育部高等学校高职高专英语类专业教学指导委员会的悉心指导,由教指委秘书长牛健博士和副主任委员丁国声教授担任总顾问,由安徽新华学院外国语学院院长任静生教授担任总主编,国家示范性高等职业院校芜湖职业技术学院、安徽水利水电职业技术学院、安徽职业技术学院、安庆职业技术学院等院校的英语教学专家负责编写任务;明尼苏达大学商业管理Brian Meyer博士以及天津外国语大学等院校的专家为此套教材的出版倾注了大量的心血;其他参编人员及编辑老师们也付出了巨大的努力,在此谨向他们表示衷心的感谢。

高职高专英语教学任重道远,教材建设未有止境。本套教材的出版旨在探索新形势下高职高专英语教学的一条教学新路。缺点与不足之处在所难免,衷心希望得到专家学者的批评指正,听到广大师生的改进意见。

编者
2014年1月

Contents

Unit 1　Business Trip **1**
　　Part Ⅰ　Listening and Speaking / 2
　　Part Ⅱ　Reading / 5
　　　　　Text A　Introduction to Chinese Visa / 5
　　　　　Text B　Online Check-in Service / 9
　　Part Ⅲ　Writing: Departure Card / Arrival Card / 12
　　Part Ⅳ　Cultural Express: The Importance of Security Check / 15
　　Supplementary Vocabulary / 15

Unit 2　Hotel **17**
　　Part Ⅰ　Listening and Speaking / 18
　　Part Ⅱ　Reading / 20
　　　　　Text A　General Introduction to Hotel Management / 20
　　　　　Text B　The Front Office / 23
　　Part Ⅲ　Writing: A Hotel Reservation Card / 26
　　Part Ⅳ　Cultural Express: What's the Best Choice for Hotels / 28
　　Supplementary Vocabulary / 29

Unit 3　Banking **31**
　　Part Ⅰ　Listening and Speaking / 32
　　Part Ⅱ　Reading / 35
　　　　　Text A　Electronic Banking / 35
　　　　　Text B　Credit Card / 39
　　Part Ⅲ　Writing: Payment Reminder / 42
　　Part Ⅳ　Cultural Express: Many Ways to Bank Online / 46
　　Supplementary Vocabulary / 47

Unit 4   Supermarket 49

  Part Ⅰ   Listening and Speaking / 50
  Part Ⅱ   Reading / 52
            Text A   TESCO / 52
            Text B   The Department Store / 55
  Part Ⅲ   Writing: Complaints and Claims/ 58
  Part Ⅳ   Cultural Express: Factory outlets / 60
  Supplementary Vocabulary / 61

Unit 5   Enterprise 62

  Part Ⅰ   Listening and Speaking / 63
  Part Ⅱ   Reading / 65
            Text A   Introduction of Apple Inc. / 66
            Text B   How to Face Your First Day Like a Pro / 69
  Part Ⅲ   Writing: A Company Profile / 71
  Part Ⅳ   Cultural Express: Wal-Mart's Influence Grows/ 72
  Supplementary Vocabulary / 74

Unit 6   Business Contact 75

  Part Ⅰ   Listening and Speaking / 76
  Part Ⅱ   Reading / 81
            Text A   Red Bull Gives You a Business Strategy / 81
            Text B   Ten Ways to Handle Customer's Complaint / 84
  Part Ⅲ   Writing: Memo / 87
  Part Ⅳ   Cultural Express: How to Form a Business Partnership / 89
  Supplementary Vocabulary / 90

Unit 7   Automobile 91

  Part Ⅰ   Listening and Speaking / 92
  Part Ⅱ   Reading / 94
            Text A   Audi's New Dynamism / 94
            Text B   You Should Think About a Job Selling Cars / 98
  Part Ⅲ   Writing: Table/Graph Composition / 101
  Part Ⅳ   Cultural Express: Beetle — 2014 VW Beetle Features — Volkswagen of America / 104
  Supplementary Vocabulary / 105

● *Contents* ●

Unit 8　E-commerce ·· **107**

　　Part Ⅰ　Listening and Speaking / 108
　　Part Ⅱ　Reading / 111
　　　　　　Text A　*Introduction to E-business* / 111
　　　　　　Text B　*E-Money* / 114
　　Part Ⅲ　Writing: Orders / 117
　　Part Ⅳ　Cultural Express: Internet Marketing / 121
　　Supplementary Vocabulary / 122

Unit 1

Business Trip

Learning Objectives:

You are able to:

☞ Understand the basic meaning about passports and visas

☞ Learn how to arrange a business trip

☞ Know how to choose the proper Airline Company and book tickets by phone or online

☞ Get to know how to fill in the departure card and arrival card

Language Focus

aircraft /plane	飞机
check in	办理登机手续(ID, passport, ticket or e-ticket)
boarding pass/card	登机牌
delay	航班延误
air traffic controller	空中交通管制员(空管)
baggage handler	行李管理员/分拣员
first/business/economy class	头等/商务/经济舱
flight attendant/cabin crew	空中乘务人员/机组人员
one way/round (return) trip ticket	单程/双程票

Part I Listening and Speaking

Task 1 Listening Practice

Exercise 1 Reserving two seats to New York

Directions: Now you will hear a short dialogue. Listen carefully and choose the best answer from the four choices.

1. How many tickets does the speaker reserve in their dialogue?
   A) One.   B) Two.   C) Three.   D) Four.
2. What kind of class does he want to choose?
   A) First class.   B) Second class.   C) Business class.   D) Economy class.
3. When does the speaker arrive in New York?
   A) 10: 25.   B) 10: 35.   C) 10: 45.   D) 10: 30.
4. How much does he spend on the one-way trip?
   A) 400$.   B) 315$.   C) 300$.   D) 350$.

Exercise 2 Checking in at the airport

Directions: Now you will hear a conversation. You are required to put in the missing information.

W: Your ticket, please. A window or aisle seat, sir?
M: _____, please. Also, I'd like a seat in the _____ section.
W: Please put your things on the scale.
M: OK. I hope my bags aren't _____.
W: No, you're OK. Here's your _____, sir.
M: What gate do I go to?
W: You'll be boarding from gate _____.
M: Thanks a lot.
W: Have a good flight, sir.

Exercise 3 A dialogue at the customhouse between Frank and a clerk

Directions: Now you will hear a conversation. You are required to put in the missing information.

Clerk: Good afternoon. Welcome to America.
Frank: Thanks.
Clerk: May I see your passport and customs declaration form?
Frank: Yes, here they are.
Clerk: Thank you. What's your _____?
Frank: I'm a driver.
Clerk: What's the purpose of your visit?
Frank: Business.

Clerk:	Where are you staying?
Frank:	I will stay at Boston Hotel.
Clerk:	Do you have a return ticket to Taiwan?
Frank:	Yes, here it is.
Clerk:	How much money do you have with you?
Frank:	I have 800 dollars.
Clerk:	Good. Have a nice day.
Frank:	Thank you.
Clerk:	Your forms are all right. I will return your _____ to you. Please keep them with you and take them here when you leave the States.
Frank:	Ok, thanks.
Clerk:	Do you have anything to declare?
Frank:	No, these are gifts for my friends.
Clerk:	I'm sorry. I'm afraid I'll have to check this _____.
Frank:	Just my camera and personal things. How about my backpack?
Clerk:	Open that too, please. What's in the plastics, sir?
Frank:	Am I _____ to bring in the fruit?
Clerk:	Sorry, perishables are not allowed. Don't you have anything more to declare?
Frank:	No I don't.
Clerk:	Excuse me, (Pointing to the handbag) would you open this bag, please?
Frank:	Sure.
Clerk:	Are these yours?
Frank:	Yes, these are my personal stuff.
Clerk:	Are you bringing in any liquor?
Frank:	No, I'm not.
Clerk:	Are you bringing in any _____?
Frank:	Only my own use.
Clerk:	All right. Please open your bags.
Clerk:	Thank you. Have a good stay in New York.
Frank:	Thank you.

Exercise 4   Checking the departure time.

Directions: Now you will hear a short dialogue. Listen carefully and decide whether the following statements are true or false.

_____ 1. The passenger's flight will be departing on time.

_____ 2. The passenger doesn't know when he will be boarding.

_____ 3. He stays in the lobby waiting for his flight.

_____ 4. He will wait for about 14 minutes.

_____ 5. There is an announcement to inform the passengers of flight.

Task 2 Oral Practice

Exercise 1

Directions: Read the following dialogue about the first business trip and find the proper words to complete each sentence.

Jean: Hey Kyle, guess what! The boss is sending me to the West Coast for a marketing seminar next month.

Kyle: Ah hah, you must be happy. You've been itching to go on a business trip for months.

Jean: Yeah, and he said there'll be more coming up, so I should get a corporate card. Problem is, I don't know how to proceed, and I didn't want the boss to know that. Can you fill me in?

Kyle: Sure, no problem. First, go see the secretary and tell her where you're going and when. She'll arrange for transportation and hotel through our travel agent, and give you the tickets and itinerary in a few days. At the same time, ask her for an application form for the card.

Jean: Will I use the card for everything?

Kyle: No, we have company credit arrangements with some major airlines and hotels. For this trip, you'll probably only use it for food. Not all restaurants accept the card, so you may have to pay cash.

Jean: Do I pay out of my own pocket?

Kyle: Afraid so. We used to have cash advances, but the company stopped that when they started issuing cards.

Jean: Will the company reimburse everything?

Kyle: No, there are maximum per diem rates. I'll give you a list. Of course, personal items aren't covered. And make sure you keep all your receipts. You'll have to attach them to your expense account when you get back.

Jean: Anything else?

Kyle: Since you'll be traveling often, apply for a frequent flyer card. Gathering frequent flyer miles is one of the perks of business travel. And let me know how you like living out of a suitcase.

> * reimburse 报销,偿还 be itching to do something 迫不及待地去做某事
>   per diem 每日,按日 receipt 收据,发票

1. You should see the secretary and tell her _____ you're going and _____. She'll arrange for transportation and hotel through _____.

2. The function of company credit is _____.

3. The company will not reimburse everything, and your personal items aren't included. So, you should keep all your _____.

4. If you often fly here and there, you will try to gather _____.

Exercise 2

Direction: Work in groups. Look at the list of business preparations for international travel. You will interview your partners to ask them to choose the three most important tips for the business traveler and explain the reasons.

> *Language differences
> *Seasonal weather conditions in the countries to be visited
> * Health care (e.g. what to eat, special medical problems and prescription drugs)
> * Electrical current (e.g. a transformer or plug adapter)
> * Money (e.g. exchanging currency and using credit cards or travelers' checks)
> * Transportation, accommodation and communication
> * Cultural differences
> * Tipping

Part II Reading

Text A

Before Reading:
1. What should you do if you want to go abroad?
2. Do you know what Visa is? What passport is?

Introduction to Chinese Visa

A Chinese visa is a permit issued by the Chinese visa authorities to an alien for entry into, exit from or transit through China. The Chinese visa authorities may issue a Diplomatic, Courtesy, Service or Ordinary Visa to an alien according to his status, purpose of visit to China or passport type. The Ordinary Visa consists of eight sub-categories, which are respectively marked with Chinese phonetic letters D, F, G, L, X, Z, C and J.

~ Tourist Visa (L Visa) is issued to an alien who comes to China temporarily for tourism, sightseeing, visits with friends or relatives, medical treatment or other private purposes. China tourist visa is valid for 6 months with single-entry, or 6 months with double-entry, or 6 months/12 months with multiple-entry.

~ Business Visa (F Visa) is issued to an alien who is invited to China for a business visit, research, lecture, scientific/technological and cultural exchanges, attending professional or business convention, or short-term studies for a period of no more than six months. China business visa is valid for 6 months with single-entry, 6 months with double-entry, or 6 months/12 months with multiple-entry.

~ Work Visa (Z Visa) is issued to foreigners who enter China for a post or employment (such as teacher), and their accompanying family members. The holder of a work visa shall go through residential formalities in the local public security department within thirty days of entry into China.

~ Study Visa (X Visa) is issued to an alien who comes to China for study, advanced studies or intern practice for a period of more than six months. If the study period is no more than six months, then the applicant shall apply for a business visa (type F).

~ Transit Visa (G Visa) is issued to aliens who transit through China. U.S. passport holders must obtain a transit visa to transit through all Chinese airports except Pudong International Airport in Shanghai.

~ Resident Visa (D Visa) is issued to an alien who goes to reside permanently in China.

~ Crew Visa (C Visa) is issued to a crew member of an international train, airliner or vessel who is a foreign citizen and comes to China for business.

~ Journalist Visa (J-1, J-2 Visa) J-1 Visa is issued to a resident foreign journalist in China and his/her accompanying spouse and minor children. J-2 Visa is issued to a foreign journalist who visits China for temporary news coverage.

Visas are not required of aliens, who hold final destination tickets and have booked seats on international airliners flying directly through China, and will stay in a transit city for less than 24 hours without leaving the airport.

Visas are not required of Citizens of the following countries, who transit through Pudong Airport or Hongqiao Airport of Shanghai, provided they hold valid passports, visas for the onward countries, final destination tickets and have booked seats, and stay in Shanghai for less than 48 hours: Republic of Korea, United States, Canada, Australia, New Zealand, Germany, France, Netherlands, Belgium, Luxemburg, Portugal, Spain, Italy, Austria, Greece.

Unit 1 Business Trip

New Words

permit	/pəˈmɪt/	n.	许可证,特许证(尤指限期的)
		v.	允许;准许
issue	/ˈɪʃuː, ˈɪsjuː/	v.	公布,发表,发给
		n.	问题,议题
diplomatic	/dɪpləˈmætɪk/	adj.	外交的,古字体的;老练的
courtesy	/ˈkɜːtɪsi/	n.	礼貌,好意
respectively	/rɪˈspɛktɪvli/	adv.	分别地,各自地
phonetic	/fəˈnɛtɪk/	adj.	语音的,拼音的
temporarily	/ˈtɛmp(ə)r(ər)ɪli, ˈtɛmp(ə)ˈrɛrɪli/	adv.	暂时地;临时地
sightseeing	/ˈsʌɪtsiːɪŋ/	n.	观光,游览
valid	/ˈvalɪd/	adj.	有效的;有根据的;合法的;正当的
convention	/kənˈvɛnʃ(ə)n/	n.	大会;协定;惯例;公约
formality	/fɔːˈmalɪti/	n.	礼节,程序,拘谨
intern	/ˈɪntɜːn/	n.	实习生
transit	/ˈtransɪt, ˈtrɑːns-, -nz-/	n.	经过,通过,过境
		v.	过境
obtain	/əbˈteɪn/	v.	获得;赢得

Phrases and Expressions

entry into	进入,参加
exit from	从……退出,从……离开
consist of	由……构成
public security department	公安机关
apply (to sb/sth) (for sth)	申请,请求

Proper Names

Netherlands	/ˈnɛðələndz/	荷兰
Belgium	/ˈbɛldʒəm/	比利时
Luxemburg	/ˈlʌksəmbɜːg/	卢森堡
Portugal	/ˈpɔːtjʊg(ə)l, ˈpɔːtʃʊ-/	葡萄牙
Austria	/ˈɒstrɪə/	奥地利

Exercises

I. Answer the following questions according to the passage.

1. What is Chinese Visa?

2. How many kinds of Chinese Visa according to the passage?

3. How long can you stay in China when you hold the Business Visa?

4. What should you do if you study no more than six months in China?

5. What qualifications are required for aliens who take planes directly through China without Chinese Visa?

II. Fill in the blanks with the proper words and expressions given below, changing the form if necessary.

| transit | issue | convention | intern | reside |
| formality | permit | obtain | sightseeing | valid |

1. Let's skip the _____ and get down to business.
2. I was an administrative _____ with the Lenovo last summer.
3. Passengers right now will be able to _____ and depart the U. S. with some additional inspections and security evaluations.
4. This train ticket is _____ for three days.
5. Visitors are not _____ to touch the statues.
6. New members will be _____ with a temporary identity card.
7. Do you have a chance to do any _____?
8. She is very _____ in her views.
9. He returned to Britain in 1939, having _____ abroad for many years.
10. I finally managed to _____ a copy of the report.

III. Translate the following sentences into Chinese.

1. The Ordinary Visa consists of eight sub-categories, which are respectively marked with Chinese phonetic letters D, F, G, L, X, Z, C and J.
2. The holder of a work visa shall go through residential formalities in the local public security department within thirty days of entry into China.

3. U.S. passport holders must obtain a transit visa to transit through all Chinese airports except Pudong International Airport in Shanghai.
4. Study (X) Visa is issued to an alien who comes to China for study, advanced studies or intern practice for a period of more than six months.

IV. Translate the following sentences into English.
1. 他已向银行请求贷款。(*apply*)
2. 他家住在纽约已十余年了。(*reside*)
3. 没有许可证不准入内。(*permit*)
4. 如果此项研究结果有效,那么将是医学界一次惊人的进展。(*valid*)

Text B

Before Reading:
1. Have you ever taken plane to travel?
2. Do you know how to book flight tickets?

Online Check-in Service

Online check-in is a service that gives a possibility to check-in online to all passengers who have a ticket reservation before arriving at the airport. Passengers can enjoy check-in and select the seat from 24 hours up to 90 minutes prior to the departure time through Online Check-in web page of each Airline Company. It can be reached via internet. Simply entering your name, surname and flight details, you'll be able to check-in online. To get more detail about online check-in, "Check In Help" link can be used.

Online check-in is available for the passengers with or without baggage. It is not need to register your baggage details while check-in. Baggage check-in process might be completed at the airport "baggage drop off point" or "online check-in desk". Desks are closed 45 minutes to international, 30 minutes to domestic flights schedule departing time. In case of excess baggage, passengers have to consider the time will be spent for excess baggage payment process. The Airline Company is not responsible for probable passenger delays due to excess baggage process.

Passengers without baggage and have online printed boarding card may directly go to the gate through to security control or otherwise baggage should be registered at "baggage drop off point" or "online check-in desk".

If you have already seat assignment in your reservation record, Online Check-in process will be completed accordingly then seat change facility can be used if it is requested. By using online check-in link user could login on system and by using "seat change" button, the process can be completed. Please be aware however, that additional airport security screening measures may increase the time required to complete the check-in process at the airport.

New Words

reservation	/rezə'veɪʃ(ə)n/	n.	预约,预订;保留
select	/sɪ'lekt/	v.	挑选;选拔
baggage	/'bægɪdʒ/	n.	行李
register	/'redʒɪstə/	v.	登记;记录;注册;挂号
		n.	登记簿;记录;暂存器
excess	/'ɛksɛs/	adj.	过量的;额外的
assignment	/ə'sʌnm(ə)nt/	n.	分配;任务;功课;委派
facility	/fə'sɪlɪti/	n.	设备;设施;才能;资质;灵巧;熟练

Phrases and Expressions

be available for	对什么来说有用的
baggage drop off point	行李放落点
online check-in desk	在线登机柜台
in case of	假如,万一
security control	安检

Exercises

I. Read the above passage carefully and decide whether the following statements are true or false.

_____ 1. Online check-in is a service that gives a possibility to check-in online to all passengers who have a ticket reservation before arriving at the airport.

_____ 2. The earliest time for check-in is 12 hours prior to the departure time, and the latest time is 90 minutes prior to the departure time.

_____ 3. Simply entering your name and you'll be able to check-in online.

_____ 4. You should go to "baggage drop off point" or "online check-in desk" to check in your baggage.

_____ 5. You should login on the online check-in user system by using "seat change" button to change your seat.

• Unit 1 Business Trip •

II. Fill in the blanks with the proper words and expressions given below, changing the form if necessary.

select	reservation	register	excess	available
in case of	prior to	facility	assignment	due to

1. His success is entirely _____ his hard work.
2. You'd better remember the way to the entrance _____ emergency.
3. He is officially _____ as disabled.
4. Tickets _____ at ticket windows.
5. These oranges have been carefully _____.
6. All the arrangements should have been completed _____ our departure.
7. He has just finished a difficult _____.
8. Luggage in _____ of 20kg is taxed.
9. Have you made the _____ for our holiday yet?
10. It describes completely the _____ and its safety basis.

III. Pay attention to different parts of speech and select the appropriate word to fill in the blank.

1. reserve, reservation, reserved
   a. Bob is very _____ — you never know what he's thinking.
   b. We accept their offer without _____.
   c. We must keep back a _____ of foods.
2. depart, departure, department
   a. On this occasion we _____ from our normal practice of holding the meetings in public.
   b. She is the head of the firm's personnel _____.
   c. What is the _____ time of the flight to New York?
3. use, used, useful, useless
   a. It's _____ to complain.
   b. We _____ the money to buy a car.
   c. She is a _____ person to know.
   d. I'm not _____ to spicy food.
4. assign, assignment, assignable
   a. His _____ was to follow the spy.
   b. We _____ a day for our meeting.
   c. This Guarantee is divisible, transferable and _____ without presentation of it to us.
5. in case, in case of, in any case
   a. _____ fire, ring the bell.
   b. Take your coat _____ it rains.
   c. The cost maybe lower than we first thought, but _____ it will still be substantial.

IV. Class Work

Discuss with your partner and tell us what the best air travel is according to your imagination or your experience.

Part III Writing

Departure Card / Arrival Card

A **departure card**, also known as an outgoing passenger card or embarkation card, is a legal document used by immigration authorities to provide passenger identification and an effective record of a person's departure from certain countries. It also serves as a declaration in relation to health and character requirements for non-citizens entering a particular country. The departure card can come attached with its corresponding arrival card with the former being retained in the passport after passport control clearance. The card is then surrendered to passport control upon departure.

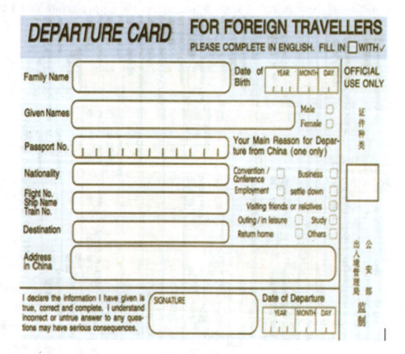

Typically the information on the departure card includes

- Full name
- Nationality
- Passport number
- Flight number or name of aircraft, ship or vehicle

- Purpose of trip: vacation, education/study, visiting relatives/families, business, diplomatic
- Duration of stay
- Destination (next stop of disembarkation)
- Address in country

Travelers are also required to sign, date and declare the information is true, correct and complete.

Passengers on international flights required to fill in departure cards need a valid boarding pass and Passport to proceed through immigration checkpoints.

An **arrival card** is a legal document used by immigration authorities to provide passenger identification and a record of a person's entry into certain countries. It also provides information on health and character requirements for non-citizens entering a particular country. Some countries such as the United States and Singapore attach the card to a departure card where the latter is retained in the alien's passport until his eventual departure. The arrival card can also be combined with items found in a customs declaration card which some countries require incoming passengers to fill out separately.

An arrival card may also be known as an incoming passenger card, landing card or disembarkation card.

The information requested varies by country.

Typically the information requested on the arrival card includes:
- Full name
- Nationality
- Date of Birth
- Passport number, place of issuance and expiry date
- Flight number or name of aircraft, ship or vehicle
- Purpose of trip: vacation, education/study, visiting relatives/families, business, diplomatic
- Duration of stay
- Destination (next stop of disembarkation)
- Address in country

Information on items being bought into the country which may be of interest to customs and quarantine authorities.

Travelers are generally required to sign, date, and declare the information is true, correct, and complete.

Passengers on international flights are often required to complete the cards and are often required to present the cards and their passports at immigration checkpoints. Some countries, most notably those in the Schengen Zone don't require aliens to complete this card.

Departure Card

For immigration clearance

Family name _____

Given name _____

Passport No. _____

Date of birth_____(Year)_____(Month)_____(Day)   Male   Female

Flight No./Ship' name/Train No. _____

Nationality _____

　　I hereby declare that the statement given above is true and accurate,

Signature_____

Retain this card in your possession; failure to do so may delay your departure from China.

Arrival Card

Family name _____   Given name _____

Nationality _____   Passport No._____

Address in China_____   Male _____ Female _____

Date of birth_____   Purpose of visit (one only)

Visa No._____   Conference/Business___ Visit___Sightseeing___

Place of Visa Issuance_____   Visiting friends____Employment____Study____

Flight No./Ship's name/Train No._____   Return home____Settle down____other____

　　I hereby declare that the statement given above is true and accurate.

Signature_____

Part IV Cultural Express

The Importance of Security Check

As a result of the airplane hijackings that have taken place with increasing frequency, almost all airports all over the world have instituted pre-boarding security checks for weapons and even, in some places, for potentially dangerous or demented persons. These procedures usually consist of a baggage search and some sort of personal search for concealed weapons. And this is ordinarily done with an electronic metal detector.

In almost all cases, the actual search is carried out by government agents rather than airline personnel. A few passengers will complain about it in no uncertain terms. The point that the agent must make, of course, is that the search is being made for the passenger's own protection. Most passengers will readily accept this fact and endure the brief unpleasantness with good humor. And the fact is, the security regulations have really worked. Hijacking has been cut to zero or near zero in those countries with the strictest regulations.

Supplementary Vocabulary

Customs Declaration Form	报关单
check in luggage	托运行李
carry-on luggage	随身携带的行李
luggage allowance	行李限额
registration form	登记表
receipt	收据
duty-free	免税
duty-free shop / store	免税店
pay duty on	为……纳税
declare	申报
itinerary	行程表
cash advance	预支费用
expense account	报销单
reimbursement	公司所返还的差旅费
living out of a suitcase	旅行包生活（长时间在旅途中而不在家中，在旅行带上所有的日常必需品，而不能享受家的舒适。）
length of stay	停留时间

perks	额外津贴
per diem rate	每日定额(公司对员工公务旅行每日花费的定额标准,包括酒店费用和餐饮费用等。)
frequent flyer miles	航空积分里程
Red Passage	红色通道(所谓"红色通道"也称"申报"通道,是指须经过海关履行检查和检验手续后,方可放行的通道)

Unit 2

Hotel

Learning Objectives:

You are able to:

☞ Be familiar with hotel facilities and hotel clerks

☞ Be acquainted with hotel procedures

☞ Use the proper expressions to carry out hotel procedures

☞ Write reservation cards

Language Focus

hotel	酒店,宾馆,旅馆,饭店		
hostel	旅社,招待所;(英)大学宿舍,(英古)旅馆		
motel	也作 motor hotels 汽车旅馆		
inns	小旅馆,客栈		
lodge	乡间小屋,旅社		
resort	度假胜地,度假村		
single bed	单人床	twin beds	两张单人床
double bed	双人床	queen size bed	加大双人床
king size bed	特大号床	receptionist	接待员
switchboard operators	接线员	a bell-man	也作 a bell-boy 门童
resident manager	客房部经理	the front desk	前台
lounges	大堂	a single room	单人间
a double room	双人间		

Part I Listening and Speaking

Task 1 Listening Practice

Exercise 1

Directions: Now you will hear a short dialogue. Listen carefully and choose the best answer from the four choices.

1. James is a _____.
   A. receptionist   B. guest   C. bellman
2. Mr. Smith's room is _____.
   A. 1023   B. 1203   C. 1320
3. James helps Mr. Smith take his _____.
   A. key   B. luggage   C. Bag
4. James show Mr. Smith to _____.
   A. his room   B. the dining hall   C. the reception desk

Exercise 2

Directions: Now you will hear a conversation. You are required to put in the missing information.

M: Excuse me, can you show ___1___ for me?
W: Yes. Follow me, please. This is your ___2___. It's also your room card.
M: Oh, I see. It's ___3___ card.
W: Yes, sir. This is your room.
M: Looks ___4___.
W: If you need anything, just call ___5___.
M: Thanks.

Exercise 3

Directions: Now you will hear a conversation. You are required to put in the missing information.

A: ___1___, may I come in?
B: Come in, please.
A: What's ___2___, sir?
B: The ___3___ doesn't flush.
A: Let me see. Oh, it's clogged. It's ___4___ now. You can try it.
B: Yes, it's ___5___ now.
A: If you need any other thing, please let us now.
B: Yes, I will.

Exercise 4

Directions: Now you will hear a short passage. Listen carefully and decide whether the following statements are true or false.

_____ 1. A receptionist's only job is to register the guest.
_____ 2. It's not necessary for a receptionist to answer the guest's phones.
_____ 3. The bellman gives the guest's their room keys.
_____ 4. A receptionist should explain the hotel's services to the guests.
_____ 5. A receptionist should wish the guest a enjoyable stay at the hotel.

Task 2 Oral Practice

Directions: Learn to communicate in the given situations and make a conversation between a guest and a receptionist according to the following requirements.

A guest steps in to ask for a room for the night, which he hasn's reserved in advance. The receptionist says she can arrange a room for him only after seven o'clock that evening or recommend some other hotels. The guest prefers to wait.

Task 3 Class Work

Now you see a brief introduction of a hotel.

Everlyn Hall

Accommodation

122 rooms, six conference rooms accommodating up to 200 delegates; 24-hour room service, and free parking.

Sports and recreation

Indoor pool, health club, nearby golf course

Getting to the hotel

Only 10 minutes from Leeds Airport and an hour from Manchester Airport

Room rates

£69 weekends; £54 Monday to Friday

Exercise:

Suppose you are the receptionist of this hotel. A guest calls for information about your hotel. Be prepared to answer his or her questions.

Part II Reading

Text A

Before Reading:
1. If you are the general manager of a hotel, how will you manage it?
2. Have you stayed in a western hotel? How do you feel about it?

General Introduction to Hotel Management

Hotel management is a complex process. It involves planning, organization, administration, controlling and coordination of a variety of resources, say, personnel, finance, material goods and information. Hotel management is, in the first place, an economic activity with the double efficiency objectives, both economically and socially. Furthermore, hotel management is more likely to be an active coordination between inner and outer resources to achieve balance. Hotel management, therefore, carries five basic functions, namely, "planning, organization, administration, coordination and controlling" respectively.

1. Planning: This function concerns estimating future tendency on the basis of close investigation, setting up objectives, and afterwards formulating a detailed schedule to fulfill those already-made objectives. Planning stands at the doorway of hotel management and ensures timely solution to any questions coming up in the process of management.

2. Organization: It refers to the establishment of efficient management system with a view to making good use of hotel resources. Organization could be interpreted on four different layers. For one, it is a feasible organization structure with clear-cut departments and management levels; also it means a whole and effective system in which definite duties and rights of different units are allocated and coordinated with harmony; thirdly, all hotel resources are organized and adjusted with real need in each period; and lastly, that is the general organization of overall activities and separate activities.

3. Administration: This function aims to promote the activities of separate departments and persons under the orders given by superiors. The order or instruction, reflecting the general decision of the hotel, is carried out in the form of language, either oral or written by one or several managerial personnel. Administration differs at different positions. Strategic decisions belong to top management while partial decisions are made on department level, as are supposed to be timely, exact and plenty.

4. Coordination: Managerial personnel make an effort to adjust and interrelate different business operations within the hotel to ensure all departments to develop harmoniously for the overall objectives. To realize this, there are two necessary synchronisms. One is personnel, that is, to coordinate personnel relationship. Interests of single department or unit often outweigh overall goals due to different views people hold. Several ways are available to settle this issue, say, communication, discussion and even rules designed for coordination. The other synchronism is required for operation, as different department or unit cannot be sure to work with the uniform rhythm as they are doing something of different nature and requirement. Such synchronism may be achieved by coordinating effort in terms of work quantity, procedures, operation rules and environment.

5. Controlling: It is to inspect and supervise how well the planning has been going on, as is crucial for the accomplishment of objectives. With this function, potential and real problems could be promptly ratified. Controlling is put into operation throughout the whole business process, consisting of pre-, mid- and post- controlling. Pre-controlling is to eliminate foreseeable problems before operation begins and take precautions. Mid-controlling is based on efficient feedback system to spot and rectify problems promptly while the operation is going on. Post-controlling is undertaken when the operation comes to an end. Business results are compared with already-made standards, and in case of deviation, redemption methods should be rightly available.

New Words

involve	/ɪnˈvɒlv/	v.	包含；使参与，牵涉
furthermore	/fəˈðəˈmɔː/	adv.	此外；而且；与此同时；再者
estimate	/ˈɛstɪmeɪt/	v.	估计；评价，评估
formulate	/ˈfɔːmjʊleɪt/	v.	构想出，规划；确切地阐述；用公式表示
fulfill	/fʊlˈfɪl/	v.	执行(命令等)；达到(目的)；使结束
feasible	/ˈfiːzɪb(ə)l/	adj.	可行的；可用的；可实行的；可能的
harmony	/ˈhɑːməni/	n.	协调；融洽；一致；和谐
reflect	/rɪˈflɛkt/	v.	反射，反照；表达；显示
strategic	/strəˈtiːdʒɪk/	adj.	战略性的；有战略意义的；至关重要的
interrelate	/ɪntərɪˈleɪt/	v.	相互关联[影响]
ensure	/ɪnˈʃɔː/	v.	确保；担保获得[避免]
synchronism	/ˈsɪŋkrənɪz(ə)m/	n.	同期性；同步性
rhythm	/ˈrɪð(ə)m/	n.	节奏，韵律；节拍
procedure	/prəˈsiːdʒə/	n.	程序，手续；工序，过程，步骤
accomplishment	/əˈkʌmplɪʃm(ə)nt/	n.	成就；完成
eliminate	/ɪˈlɪmɪneɪt/	v.	排除，消除；除掉
foreseeable	/fɔːˈsiːəbl/	adj.	可预见到的

Phrases and Expressions	
refer to	指的是
put into operation	实施；
consist of	由……组成

Exercises

I. Answer the following questions according to the passage.

1. What is hotel management?
   _____

2. What are the five basic functions hotel management carries?
   _____

3. What does planning concern in hotel management?
   _____

4. What does organization refer to?
   _____

5. What does administration aim to do?
   _____

II. Fill in the blanks with the proper words and expressions given below, changing the form if necessary.

estimate	fulfill	feasible	reflect
ensure	put into operation	consist of	eliminate

1. That may be fine for the US, but it's not _____ for a mass European market
2. Concern at the economic situation was _____ in the government's budget.
3. The President's Council _____ the supremacy of the National Party.
4. The entire world _____ matter.
5. The Sex Discrimination Act has not _____ discrimination in employment.
6. The plan began to be _____.
7. This company should be able to _____ our requirements
8. Try to _____ how many steps it will take to get to a close object

III. Translate the following sentences into Chinese.

1. It involves planning, organization, administration, controlling and coordination of a variety of resources, say, personnel, finance, material goods and information.

2. Hotel management is, in the first place, an economic activity with the double efficiency objectives, both economically and socially.
3. It is to inspect and supervise how well the planning has been going on, as is crucial for the accomplishment of objectives.
4. Post-controlling is undertaken when the operation comes to an end.

IV. Translate the following sentences into English.
1. 规划涉及在严密的调查的基础上估计未来的趋势。
2. 管理人员努力确保所有部门的和谐发展。
3. 事前控制是消除操作前可预见的问题并采取预防措施。
4. 投产控制贯穿整个业务流程。

Text B

Before Reading:
1. Can you list the main departments in a hotel?
2. Which department is the most important?

The Front Office

The front office is not only the hotel's "shop window" but also its "nerve center". It is often said that, to the guest, the front office is the hotel.

The main duties carried out by the front office are receiving reservations, checking guests in, assigning rooms, distributing baggage, storing guests' valuables, providing information, delivering mails and messages, exchanging foreign currencies, checking room occupancies, checking guests out and so on.

Computerized property management systems have simplified checking-in. For example, with a program called "First 10", Marriott experts to cut checks-in time from 3 minutes to one-and-a-half. Hilton is implementing a similar program called "Zip-in and Check-in". At Hyatt Hotels, guests can even check in by phone before they arrive at the hotel.

Checking out has also benefited from computer technology. For example, the Milford Plaza Hotel in New York city has installed check-out stations in their lobby that are similar to the cash dispensing automatic teller machines that banks use. Guests can use the machine to check out and get a copy of their bills.

Another important duty performed at the front desk is the night audit. This is usually done between 11 p.m. and 6 a.m., when there are few other distracting duties. In a small hotel, the front desk agent on duty performs the night audit. In a larger hotel, an auditor from the accounting division usually is assigned the task. If the hotel does not have a computerized property management system, the night auditor's job can be tough, since it involves a lot of details. The night auditor must verify that guest charges have accurately posted to each guests account and that the income is properly credited to the division that earned it. This can be tedious work, especially since it involves checking for errors.

New technology has made possible the change of one of the functions of the front desk staff in some hotels—relaying messages to guests. For instance, Boston's Park Plaza has a voice-mail system. Each guest's electronic mailbox is capable of holding as many as 25 phone messages. By dialing a three-digit number on the phone in their rooms, guests can retrieve these messages. If they wish, the messages can be repeated, saved, or deleted with the touch of a button. The hotel estimates that this automated system, which relieves front desk personnel of handling this chore, will save them $ 50 000 annually. Other hotels have system that allows guests to display incoming phone messages on their TV screen after being alerted by a light on the telephone.

The success of a hotel is measured by its occupancy and average daily rate. Putting these two together, yield management can work out forecasts or estimates of the number of guests / rooms populated, thus occupancy rates for the future. To secure an effective yield management system, careful front office employee training is of vital importance.

New Words

assign	/əˈsʌin/	v.	分派,选派,分配
distribute	/dɪˈstrɪbjuːt/	v.	分配,散布;散发,分发
deliver	/dɪˈlɪvə/	v.	传送,投递
occupancy	/ˈɒkjəpənsi/	n.	占有,占领;居住;[物]占有率
simplify	/ˈsɪmplɪfʌɪ/	v.	简化;使单纯;使简易
implement	/ˈɪmplɪmɛnt/	v.	实施,执行;使生效,实现
audit	/ˈɔːdɪt/	n.	审计,查账
distract	/dɪˈstrakt/	v.	使分心;使混乱
auditor	/ˈɔːdɪtə/	n.	审计员;查账员
alert	/əˈlɔːt/	v.	向……报警
secure	/sɪˈkjʊə/	v.	保护;(使)获得;使安全;担保
yield	/jiːld/	n.	产量,产额;投资的收益;产品
vital	/ˈvʌɪt(ə)l/	adj.	至关重要的;生死攸关的;生气勃勃的

Unit 2 Hotel

Phrases and Expressions

automatic teller machine (abbr. ATM)　　自动取款机
make possible　　　　　　　　　　　　　使……成为可能

Exercises

I. Read the above passage carefully and decide whether the following statements are true or false.

　　____ 1. The front office in the hotel is very important.
　　____ 2. Human-control property management systems have simplified checking-in.
　　____ 3. Marriot is implementing a similar program called "Zip-in and Check-in".
　　____ 4. Another important duty performed at the front desk is the night audit which is usually done between 10 p.m. and 6 a.m..
　　____ 5. We can measure the success of a hotel by its occupancy and average daily rate.

II. Fill in the blanks with the proper words and expressions given below, changing the form if necessary.

simplify	assign	occupancy	vital	
yield	ensure	alert	deliver	distribute

1. The journal is _____ worldwide.
2. We can give you up to 28 days for _____.
3. Don't allow noise to _____ you from your work.
4. An _____ police officer discovered a lorry full of explosive.
5. Please check to _____ that all nuts and bolts are secure.
6. The land _____ grapes and tobacco.
7. Secrecy is of _____ importance
8. 70 per cent _____ is needed to give a profit
9. She has been _____ to a new job.
10. We have done our best to _____ the check-in procedure.

III. Pay attention to different parts of speech and select the appropriate word to fill in the blank.

1. assign, assigner(assignor), assignable
   a. It's wise to _____ special exercises to the weaker students.
   b. This standby letter of credit is neither _____ nor transferable.
   c. The _____ may not continue to use the assigned enterprise name after the assignment.

2. distribute, distribution, distributive

   a. The foreman _____ the work every morning.

   b. The conference discussed the fair _____ of income and wealth.

   c. Today, we turn to the question of _____ justice.

3. delivery, deliver

   a. The president will _____ a speech about schools.

   b. How much extra does _____ cost.

4. occupancy, occupy

   a. How much weight does a happy life _____?

   b. During her _____ the garden was transformed.

5. simplicity, simplify, simple

   a. Try to _____ your explanation for the children.

   b. I like her all the better for her _____.

   c. She was ashamed to ask such a _____ question.

IV. Class Work

Discuss with your partner and tell us the main duties of the front office?

Part III Writing

A Hotel Reservation Card

A hotel reservation consists of two parts: hotel's information and customer's information. Hotel's information consists of hotel's name, address, zip code and telephone number. Customer's information includes customer's name, check-in time, check-out time, room type, number of beds, smoking preference, payment, telephone number, fax and e-mail. You should note that:

1. The hotel's address and telephone should be written at the upper left corner of the application form.

2. Bed types consist of no preference, king bed, queen bed, single bed, double bed and twin beds.

3. Smoking preference includes no preference, smoking and non-smoking.

4. Payment can be divided into in cash and by credit card, etc. If the customer makes reservation online, he will be asked to pay the bill by credit card by the hotel.

• Unit 2 Hotel •

... Hotel
Hotel Reservation Card   Reservations   ... Hotel   Address   Zip code   Tel.
Guest's name: _____
Check in: _____   Check out: _____
Room type: _____   Number of beds: _____
Smoking preference: _____   Payment: _____
Tel. number: _____   Fax: _____
E-mail: _____

Sample

Holiday Hotel
Reservation Card

Reservations
Holiday Hotel
99 Changjiang Road, Hefei City
230061
0551-64689888

Guest's name: Wang Tao
Check in: 20/9/2013   Check out: 29/9/2013
Room type: double room
Number of beds: 2
Smoking preference: no preference
Payment: by traveler's check
Tel. number: 0732-8633778
Fax: 0732-8633778
E-mail: Chenting@126.com

Exercise:

Directions: Write a hotel reservation according to the information given below.

假如你叫Tom White,将于2013年12月21日到合肥出差,预计将在合肥住5天。听说合肥长江路25号的友谊宾馆环境很好,服务不错,你打算在那预订一间无烟带淋浴的单人间。你的付款方式为信用卡,联系电话:0686-3377986,传真:0686-3377986,电子邮箱:tomwhite@hotmail.com。

Part IV Cultural Express

What's the Best Choice for Hotels

The organic amenities are becoming more and more popular nowadays. But the traditional articles are also struggling in their way. But what's the best choice for hotels about them? Such as the soap, toothpaste, shower cap, gels etc. Hotel amenities come in many forms. If you consider a dry floor and a roof above your head a luxury, your life must be exciting and adventure-filled. However, if what you need to feel like you're treating yourself is an on-call concierge, towel warmers and that lovely little after-dinner mint on your pillow after turn-down service, well, hello sister! Just be sure you make your reservation at the right hotel for your own personal vacation style.

Since such features are standard at most properties, hotels distinguish themselves by focusing on outstanding service. At Keswick Hall, a colonial-style mansion at the foot of the Blue Ridge Mountains in Virginia, new mothers can call on the baby butler. This attendant warms bottles, places a rocking chair and personalized crib in the room and rocks the baby to sleep while mom soaks in the tub.

The baby butler may be a unique service, but enhanced concierge and butler programs have become an industry bellwether. Steven Ferry, chairman of the International Institute of Modern Butlers, has noticed a dramatic increase in the number of hotels adding butlers to their staff in the past four years. They are trained to handle even the slightest of needs, from drawing a bath at the perfect temperature, to serving morning tea, to laying out a guest's clothes in the morning. A properly trained butler, says Ferry, will anticipate a guest's needs and address them seamlessly.

While there are at least 150 hotel butler programs around the world, according to Ferry's organization, properties are incorporating a number of services to satisfy their guests.

Some concentrate on minor but telling details. At the Ritz Madrid in Spain, monogrammed robes are placed in a guest's room before arrival. At Jade Mountain, a Caribbean resort, a poem is placed on each pillow at turn-down sheet.

Other hotels target a specific type of guest, like the pet-owner or environmentalist.

The Lowell New York offers room service for pets, with choices like filet mignon tartar and organic buffalo marrow bone. At the Four Seasons Resort Nevis in the West Indies, guests can contribute to local conservation efforts by paying to adopt an endangered sea turtle, which has been tagged with a satellite transmitter for research purposes. Adoptive guests then monitor their turtles' migratory patterns via an Internet-based program.

Many luxury hotels have also shifted from a staid atmosphere to one that indulges their guests' interests, whether that's gourmet food or adventurous excursions.

The Enchantment Resort, a spa in Sedona, Ariz., has outfitted room terraces with built-in grills and offers an assortment of meats which are delivered by room service. At the Banyan Tree Phuket in Thailand, guests can fly by private plane to a secluded island, where they'll watch the sun rise over breakfast. This may sound unoriginal, but the most sophisticated hotels integrate a guest's every whim to make the experience truly memorable.

Such extravagances will only become more common among luxury hotels since fierce competition begets stand-out services and amenities. The hotel industry started more than a century ago when stagecoach outposts gave overland travelers a refuge from the elements — and little else. Nowadays, however, five-star properties offer well-heeled guests spa treatments, personal butlers and even room service for pets.

Such popular services and experiences could be helping keep occupancy rates high. Luxury hotels have yet to suffer from the sluggish economy, with occupancy falling just 1 percent between January and May 2008 as compared to the same time period in 2007, according to Smith Travel Research, which collects data on the lodging industry.

Supplementary Vocabulary

check in	入住登记
check out	办理退房手续
deluxe suite	豪华套间
dining hall	餐厅
double room	双人间
foreign exchange counter	外币兑换处
hotel directory	旅馆指南
hotel lobby	饭店大堂
hotel rates	房价
information desk	总台
porter	行李员

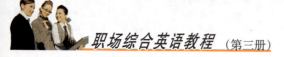

reservation desk	预定处
room charge sheet	房价表
room with bath	带有浴室的客房
room with good ventilation	通风良好的客房
single room	单人间
suite	套间
telephone operator	总机接线员
In cash	现金付款
By credit card	信用卡付款

称谓：

1. 直接称谓：Mr./ Mrs./ Miss. / Ms. XXX,
   Sir/ Madam/ Gentlemen/ Lady.
2. 间接称谓：that lady, that gentleman,
   the lady with you, the gentleman with you.

问好：

1. Good morning/ afternoon/ evening, sir/madam. 早上/下午/晚上好！先生/夫人。
2. How are you today, sir? 先生，今天一切都好吗？
   Thank you. And you? 很好，谢谢。你呢？

欢迎：

1. Welcome to the Guangdong Foreign Businessmen Club! 欢迎光临广东外商俱乐部。
2. Welcome to XX hotel! 欢迎光临XX酒店！
3. Glad to see you again. 很高兴再见到您！

询问/征询：

1. May I have your name/ room number, please? 请问您的名字/房号？
2. May I take your order now? 我现在为您下单好吗？
3. May I know who I'm talking with? 请问您是哪位？（打电话时用）
4. May I ask who is the next? 请问下一位是谁？
5. May I help you with ... madam? 夫人，我能帮您做……吗？
6. Would you like me to book ... for you? 需要我为您订……吗？
7. Would you like to sit by the window? 您喜欢坐在靠窗边的位置吗？
8. Would you like to have a cup of tea? 来杯咖啡如何？
9. Is there anything else I can do for you, madam? 这儿需要我帮忙吗？
10. How about ...? 您觉得……怎样？

祝愿/祝福：

1. Have a pleasant stay at our hotel, sir/ madam. 愿您在我们酒店一切开心！
2. Have a good/ nice/pleasant day/ evening/ weekend! 祝您今天/今晚/周末一切都好！

Unit 3

Banking

Learning Objectives:

You are able to:

☞ Be familiar with some basic daily banking procedures
☞ Use the proper expressions to carry out banking procedures
☞ Know the function of credit cards
☞ Write payment reminder
☞ Know certain information about some famous banks

Language Focus

deposit	存储,存(款)
deposit form / slip	(存款人在银行存款时填写的)存款单
receipt	发票;收据
open / close an account	开立/结清一个账户
deposit / savings / checking account	定期存款/储蓄账户/(支票)活期存款账户
annual	每年的;年度的;一年一次的
deposit / withdraw money	存钱/取钱
cash	钱(可指纸币也可指硬币);现款,现金
transfer	汇兑;转让;过户
sign one's name	签名,署名;签字
fill out	填写
the interest rate	利息率

Part I Listening and Speaking

Task 1 Listening Practice

Exercise 1 Dialogue between a clerk and Mary at a bank

Directions: Now you will hear a short dialogue. Listen carefully and choose the best answer from the four choices.

1. Mary would like to _____.
   A. deposit some money   B. borrow some money
   C. lend some money   D. set up a bank
2. Mary is required to sign on the _____.
   A. passbook   B. passport
   C. deposit receipt   D. notebook
3. Mary wants to open a _____.
   A. savings account   B. cheking account
   C. minimun account   D. deposit account
4. The annual fee for each account is _____.
   A. five yuan   B. ten yuan
   C. 300 yuan   D. one yuan

Exercise 2

Directions: Now you will hear a conversation. You are required to put in the missing information.

Mary: Oh, I'm sorry, I've forgotten to deposit 3,000 yuan into my ____1____.
Clerk: Alright, please give me your check card, passport and cash.
Mary: I want to ____2____ 10,000 yuan to my CD savings account for two years.
Clerk: OK, one moment please…Please sign your name on these sheets. Please ____3____ this deposit form, first.
Mary: OK … Here you are. Any problem on that?
Clerk: No, that's fine. Please give your ____4____ to me?
Mary: Ok. Here it is, and the cash.
Clerk: Wait a moment, please.
Mary: Sure.
Clerk: Is there anything else I can do for you?
Mary: Yes. Can you tell me what the ____5____ is now?
Clerk: The deposit rate is 0.8% every month.
Mary: Thanks.

Exercise 3

Directions: Now you will hear a conversation. You are required to put in the missing information.

Betty: Excuse me. Is this where you ____1____ foreign money for RMB?
Cashier: Yes. What can I do for you?
Betty: I'd like to change some ____2____ for RMB.
Cashier: Oh, I see. How much do you have?
Betty: 100 dollars.
Cashier: 100 dollars. Very well. Today's exchange ____3____ is 8.23 yuan RMB to one US dollar.
Betty: You mean the rate fluctuates daily?
Cashier: Yes, but they change only once a day. We have a rigid exchange control law. The official one. Well, here is 823 yuan. Please ____4____ to see if it is correct.
Betty: Yes, it's fine. One more thing, can I change my traveller's checks into RMB?
Cashier: Certainly. Today's rate is 8.36. How much do you want to change?
Betty: 500 dollars. I think I'll ____5____ in Shanghai.

Exercise 4

Directions: Now you will hear a short passage. Listen carefully and decide whether the following statements are true or false.

_____ 1. Lending money and collecting debts are a new way for bankers to do business.
_____ 2. People can borrow books from a library with the help of a credit card.
_____ 3. Customers don't have to go to the bank to pay their bills.
_____ 4. People can travel in another country comfortably with a credit card.
_____ 5. Cardholders have made big money from the credit card companies.

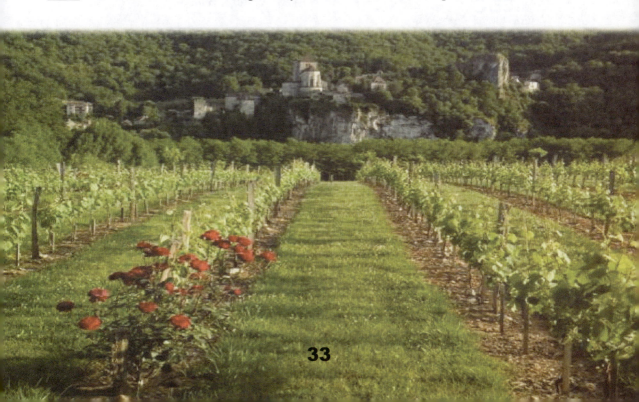

Task 2　Oral Practice

Directions: Discuss with your partner or in group to match the logos in the left column with the proper names in the right column.

(1)　　　　　　　　　　　　　A) China Construction Bank

(2)　　　　　　　　　　　　　B) Bank of China

(3)　　　　　　　　　　　　　C) Industrial and Commercial Bank of China

(4)　　　　　　　　　　　　　D) China Merchants Bank

(5)　　　　　　　　　　　　　E) People's Bank of China

(6)　　　　　　　　　　　　　F) Agricultural Bank of China

(7)　　　　　　　　　　　　　G) China Everbright Bank

(8)　　　　　　　　　　　　　H) Bank of Communications

(9)　　　　　　　　　　　　　I) CITIC Bank

Part II Reading

Text A

Before Reading:
1. What should you do if you want to save money?
2. Do you know anything about electronic banking?

Electronic Banking

It has been said that banks can be faceless institutions and, taken literally, with the progression of electronic banking, this may not be too far from the truth. Electronic banking is no longer just credit cards and automated teller machines (ATMs). Now the Internet has the technology to radically transform banking procedures, and financial institutions are taking heed with the development of the web site.

Initially, the web sites of banking institutions consisted of static web pages with no interaction between the user and the web page. The site was mainly an outlet for displaying information about the bank, its locations, and the services that it provided. Many banking web sites have evolved recently and now allow customers to perform certain transactions via the Internet, for example bill paying and checking bank balances. These advanced services have proved very popular with customers, and now with the development of new banking software applications, electronic banking will be able to account for all customers' banking needs.

BroadVision's One-To-One Financial and One-To-One Billing applications are examples of software packages that can allow financial institutions develop highly interactive web sites. It provides every customer with their own personalized web content, through a combination of business rules and customer profiles based on current and past web activity. This new approach to electronic banking has obvious advantages to both the customer and the financial institution.

The customer will now have a full suite of banking options, including bill payment transactions, customer-defined alerts, and financial management services. Financial institutions will also see the benefits of electronic banking. The new personalized service allows users to interact directly with the web site, and enter personal information and feedback. The financial institution can analyze and compile this information to learn more about their customers, and to provide a better service, leading to higher customer satisfaction. The interactivity of the site also means that customers will spend more time browsing the web site, giving financial institutions the opportunity for upselling and/or cross-selling. It will also be possible to shift certain transactions from higher-cost business channels, such as branch offices, to the low-cost Internet channel.

Security is a major concern for customers who are contemplating Internet banking. The use of firewalls, virus-protection and intrusion-detection software, and authentication has made electronic banking more secure. Data encryption has also been introduced, which guarantees that customer information is coded at all times and can only be interpreted by the relevant personnel.

In the future, electronic banking will cover all aspects of banking—even mortgages will originate online. There are already several banks that operate online only, for example Telebanc and Net.Banc, while several of the established banks, like Citibank and Chase Manhattan, have developed their electronic banking systems. Whether or not the new online banks will be able to compete with the established banks remains to be seen.

New Words

progression	/prəˈgreʃ(ə)n/	n.	前进；进展，行进
radically	/ˈrædɪk(ə)li/	adv.	根本地；彻底地，完全地；极端地；激进地
transform	/trænsˈfɔːm/	v.	使变形，使改观；改造；改善；改革
financial	/fʌɪˈnænʃ(ə)l/	adj.	财政的，金融的
heed	/hiːd/	n.	注意，留心
		v.	注意，留心；听从
static	/ˈstætɪk/	adj.	静态的；静止的
evolve	/ɪˈvɒlv/	v.	演化，发展，逐步形成
transaction	/trænˈzækʃ(ə)n/	n.	交易；业务；办理
balance	/ˈbæl(ə)ns/	n.	结存；存款余额
personalize	/ˈpəːs(ə)n(ə)lʌɪz/	v.	使针对个人，使个人化；使个性化
profile	/ˈprəʊfʌɪl/	n.	数据图表；量变曲线；人物简介；概况
option	/ˈɒpʃ(ə)n/	n.	选择；(供)选择的事物(或人)
alert	/əˈləːt/	n.	警戒(状态)，戒备(状态)
		adj.	警觉的，警惕的
feedback	/ˈfiːdbæk/	n.	反馈；反馈的信息
compile	/kəmˈpʌɪl/	v.	收集；汇编；编纂
browse	/braʊz/	v.	浏览；随便翻阅；随意观看
shift	/ʃɪft/	v.	转移；移动，改变位置(或方向)

contemplate	/ˈkɒntɛmpleɪt, -təm-/	v.	思忖,思量;对……做周密考虑
authentication	/ɔːˌθɛntɪˈkeɪʃ(ə)n/	n.	证实;认证;鉴定
encryption	/ɛnˈkrɪpʃ(ə)n/	n.	加密
mortgage	/ˈmɔːgɪdʒ/	n.	抵押;抵押借款

Phrases and Expressions

automated teller machine (ATM)	自动提款机;自动柜员机
account for	报账;(向某人)提供(钱的)开支情况
a full suite of	一整套……
compete with	(事物)媲美,比得上

Proper Names

BroadVision	美国宏道(全球著名在线电子商务和企业级社交网络的解决方案提供商)
Telebanc	美国目前资产最大的网络银行
Net.Banc	网络银行(澳大利亚网上银行控股公司)
Citibank	花旗银行(总部坐落于美国纽约派克大道399号的花旗银行是华盛顿街最古老的商业银行之一。)
Chase Manhattan	大通曼哈顿银行(美国金融业巨头之一,大型商业银行。既是大通曼哈顿(持股)公司(Chase Manhattan Corp.,1969年建立)的主要企业,又是洛克菲勒财团的金融中心。)

Exercises

I. Answer the following questions according to the passage.

1. What was the main function of the web sites of banking institutions in the early years?

2. How can a banking institution personalize its web content for a customer?

3. What banking options can be available now?

4. What are the benefits of electronic banking for both customers and financial institutions?

5. How can electronic banking be made more secure?

II. Fill in the blanks with the proper words and expressions given below, changing the form if necessary.

| radical | personalize | shift | benefit | secure |
| procedure | evolve | interaction | financial | option |

1. Attitudes towards education will have to change _____.
2. The first step in the _____ for making a kite is to build the frame.
3. Shanghai and New York are major _____ centres.
4. The games would become just another source of _____ with these e-businesses.
5. The company has _____ into a major chemical manufacturer.
6. All our courses are _____ to the needs of the individuals.
7. Students have the _____ of studying abroad in their second year.
8. I have had the _____ of a good education.
9. She _____ her weight from one foot to the other.
10. The future of the company looks _____.

III. Translate the following sentences into Chinese.
1. Electronic banking is no longer just credit cards and automated teller machines (ATMs).
2. Initially, the web sites of banking institutions consisted of static web pages with no interaction between the user and the web page.
3. This new approach to electronic banking has obvious advantages to both the customer and the financial institution.
4. Security is a major concern for customers who are contemplating Internet banking.

IV. Translate the following sentences into English.
1. 我可以点击鼠标在因特网上处理银行业务。
2. 人们认为,陆地动物由海生动物进化而成。
3. 该国正在寻找纺织品的买主。
4. 我们都很担心飞机上旅客的安全。

Text B

Before Reading:
1. Have you ever used a credit card?
2. Do you know any usage of a credit card?

Credit Card

Today, more and more people in the United States are using credit cards instead of money to buy the things they need. Almost any one who has a steady income and a continuous work record can apply for a credit card. There are many credit cards available: American Express, VISA, and Master Charge are some of the most popular.

If you have a credit card, you can buy a car, eat a dinner, take a trip, and even get a haircut by charging the cost to your account. In this way, you can pay for purchases a month later, without any extra charge. Or you may choose to make your payments over several months and pay only part of the total amount each month. If you do this, the credit company, or the bank that sponsors the credit card, will add a small service charge to your total bill. This is very convenient for the customer.

With the credit card in your wallet or purse, you don't have to carry much cash and worry about losing money through carelessness or theft. The card user only has to worry about paying the final bill. This, of course, can be a problem, if you charge more than you can pay for. In the recent years, credit cards also appear in China. The Great Wall credit card and the Peony credit card are the pioneer cards sponsored by the Bank of China and the Industrial and Commercial Bank of China, respectively.

Many of us believe that it will only be a matter of time before credit cards replace cash and checks for both individuals and businesses.

People spend a lot of money in their daily lives. Working people spend their money on transportation to and from work, and on various expenses throughout the day. Most people enjoy shopping and buy many things that they need and want. They buy sports equipment, go to sporting events, and do many things that cost money.

However, many Americans don't pay cash or write checks for these things. More and more pay for things with credit cards. Credit cards are small rectangular plastic cards. Banks give these cards to their customers. When a customer buys something at a store, he shows his card at the store. This authorizes the store to charge the bank for the customers purchase. The bank collects all the charges for each customer. Then once a month the bank requires the customer to pay all the charges for that month. The bank doesn't force the customer to pay the full amount. It allows the customer to pay for charges in several payments over a period of time. However, the bank requires the customer to pay interest on the unpaid part of the charges. In this way the bank allows customers to buy things that they can not afford at one time. People can use the cards to buy what they want and pay for it over a period of time. They also do not need to carry a lot of money.

So, a credit card is a card issued by a bank, allowing the holder to obtain goods and services on credit.

New Words

credit	/ˈkrɛdɪt/	n.	信用；信贷
apply	/əˈplʌɪ/	v.	（尤指以书面形式）申请；请求
available	/əˈveɪləb(ə)l/	adj.	可获得的，可利用的
sponsor	/ˈspɒnsə/	v.	发起；举办；资助
theft	/θɛft/	n.	偷窃；失窃
respectively	/rɪˈspɛktɪvli/	adv.	各自地，各个地，分别地
various	/ˈvɛːrɪəs/	adj.	不同的；各种各样的；
rectangular	/rɛkˈtaŋɡjʊlə/	adj.	长方形的，矩形的；像长方形的
authorize	/ˈɔːθərʌɪz/	v.	授权；委托；批准

Phrases and Expressions

instead of	代替，而不是
apply for	（尤指以书面形式）申请；请求

Proper Names

American Express	美国运通卡
VISA	维萨卡
Master Charge	万事达卡
The Great Wall credit card	长城信用卡
Peony credit card	牡丹信用卡

Exercises

I. Read the above passage carefully and decide whether the following statements are true or false.

___ 1. Today more and more Americans are using money to buy things they need.
___ 2. VISA is one of the most popular credit cards in the United States.
___ 3. If you have a credit card, you can buy a car without any charge.
___ 4. The Great Wall credit card is sponsored by the Industrial and Commercial Bank of China.
___ 5. Many people believe that credit cards will soon replace cash and checks in commerce.

II. Fill in the blanks with the proper words and expressions given below, changing the form if necessary.

apply	various	available	convenient
theft	instead of	sponsor	respectively

1. She prefers making her own clothes _____ buying them in the shops.
2. You may _____ in person or by letter.
3. Further information is _____ on request.
4. He reported the _____ of his passport to the police.
5. The church _____ the fair to raise money for elderly people.
6. It is very _____ to pay by credit card.
7. Julie Wilson and Mark Thomas, aged 17 and 19 _____.
8. There are _____ ways of doing this.

III. Pay attention to different parts of speech and select the appropriate word to fill in the blank.

1. pay (*n.*), pay (*v.*), payment, payable
   a. I don't _____ you to sit around all day doing nothing.
   b. They are finding it difficult to meet the _____ on their car.
   c. Her job is hard work, but the _____ is good.
   d. The price is _____ in monthly instalments.

2. various, variously, variety
   a. The college library has a wide _____ of books.
   b. He has been _____ described as a hero, a genius and a bully.
   c. His _____ achievements are most impressive.

3. care, careful, careless, carelessly
   a. You must be _____ when handling chemicals.
   b. Someone had _____ left a window open.
   c. Her child was her major _____.

d. It was _____ of you to leave your umbrella in the train.
4. add, addition, additional
   a. It will take an _____ two weeks to finish the work.
   b. She tasted her coffee, and then _____ more sugar.
   c. In _____ to apples you asked for, I bought you some oranges.

IV. Class Work

A reporter is interviewing the bank manager about the essential skills for using credit cards. Work in pairs and make a role play.

Part III Writing

Payment Reminder

付款催缴单是用来提醒客户缴清款项的文件。其内容有应支付的金额、货物的发票号码及其他事项。

Format (格式):
I. a template of the payment reminder sheet

REMINDER	
Your Organization Organization's Address Date: (date of issuance)	No. 0005
Description	Amount
Ref Invoice xxxx	£ xxxx
Body of the Reminder.	

II. a template of the payment reminder letter

```
                                                    Your Name
                                                    Your Organization
                                                    Organization's Address
                                                    Date: (Date of issuance of letter)

Name of Addressee
Addressee's Designation
```

Unit 3 Banking

Address

Reference: In this section you need to mention subject of the letter briefly and concisely.

Salutation/Greetings

Dear Ms./Mr. (addressee)/ To whomsoever it may concern

The first and introductory paragraph of the letter should tell the addressee why you are writing this letter. This will inform the reader that they have defaulted on their payment on the bill that was sent to them by your organization. Do mention the date on which you had sent the bill to the addressee earlier so that he or she is informed of the same. Also send a copy of the invoice with this letter so that the addressee does not have the excuse of not having the invoice and also is made aware of the overdue amount.

In the second paragraph, you need to mention details of by when your organization expects the addressee to make the payment. Mention both the amount to be paid and the date by which it needs to be paid. Also ensure that you make the addressee aware that in case the payment is not made, the addressee is liable to face legal action.

In the third paragraph, you need to assuage the fears of the addressee by saying that you believe that legal action would be completely unnecessary. Also ensure that you mention that in case the addressee has already made the payment, they should ignore this letter. Apologize for the letter in such a scenario. End the letter by giving your contact details in case the addressee needs to contact you for any kind of clarification.

Valediction/Goodbye

Yours sincerely,
(Signature)
(Your name)

Sample (范例):

I.

REMINDER	
Your Organization 10 Front Street Manchester M163XB Date: 30 June 2013 To: Ms A Bell, 69 Maple Road, Manchester.	No. 0005

Description	Amount
Ref Invoice 0002	£12
This payment is now overdue. We would be grateful if you would settle this account as soon as possible.	

II.

John Samson
Accountant, Messrs. Devon and Graham
Oak Street, Cook County
Illinois — 242574
August 18th 2010

Carla Grayson
8265 - Elm Park
Cook County
Illinois — 242897
Reference: Late Payment Reminder, Invoice # 4635789
Dear Ms Grayson,

  This letter is to remind you that as of today you have defaulted on an outstanding payment of USD 4000 on the invoice no # 4635789 which was first sent to you on the 1st of July 2010. We are yet to receive any sort of communication from you regarding the payment of that invoice. Along with this letter we have enclosed another copy of the invoice for your reference.

  We request you to kindly make the complete payment of the amount mentioned herein (USD 4000) by the 30th day of this month, that is August 30, 2010. In case you default on this payment, the company will be forced to take legal action against you to recover the payment.

  We believe that legal action would not be necessary and therefore, request you to make the payment on invoice no # 4635789 as soon as possible. In case you have already made the payment, please dismiss this letter. We apologize for the inconvenience caused in case you have already made the payment. In case you need to contact us for anything, our contact details are listed on the invoice enclosed.

  We would like to thank you for all your cooperation. Thank you for your cooperation and hope that you will continue to do business with us in the future.

  Thank you.

Yours sincerely
(Signature)
John Samson
Accountant, Messrs. Devon and Graham

Tips (写作注意事项):

A reminder letter of payment is exceptionally difficult to draft considering the fact that it must be firm yet, polite and short yet, informative. The language of the letter is another worry as it has to be formal and yet, has to be simple and plain enough to get the message across.

While writing such a letter, it is best to ascertain some facts such as date of sales, expected date of payment, grace period, etc. In addition to that, it is also important to have a look at some other facts such as the payment history of the client, total cost of goods sold, payment period and grace period permitted by your company, etc. The next concept that is to be taken into consideration is the presentation of facts, within your letter. This is best done by arranging the above mentioned facts in a chronological manner, which theoretically should go like this:

Date of purchase
Date of signing the agreement
Period of payment
Grace period
Rate of interest

The next step is of presenting these facts in a polite and courteous manner with a firm sentence construction. Remember that your sentences should never be arrogant or menacing, as it puts a blemish on your company's reputation and goodwill.

Exercise:

Directions: This part is to test your ability to do practical writing. You are required to complete the following payment reminder with the help of Chinese equivelant. Remember not to translate the Chinese word for word.

October 10, 2013

Henry Barker
Manager of The National Advertising Company
381 Fourth Avenue
Cleveland, Ohio

Dear Henry,

_____ (此信旨在告知您) that _____ (我尚未收到付款) of invoice No. 3721 for the amount of $50,000 due on October 6, 2013.

Perhaps you have overlooked the fact, but your account with us is currently overdue. I have enclosed a _____ (贵账户信息的说明). Please make your payment ASAP or give proper justification for this regard. We hope it will not be needed to _____ (再次给您发催款函).

Thank you for your prompt attention to this matter.

                                        Best Regards,
                                        [Your Signature]
                                              John Smith
                            Human Resources Department
                                    Smith & Johnson Co.
                        No. 10, Fourth Avenue, New York

Part IV Cultural Express

Many Ways to Bank Online

If you're interested in handling some of your finances online, you might not have to switch banks. Most of the country's big banks, and many of the smaller ones, have Web sites that offer at least some functionality. Brick-and-mortar banks with Web sites are sometimes called clicks-and-mortar banks. You can talk to a teller at a branch, use the bank's ATMs, call a customer-service line, and visit the bank's Web site.

Then there are the virtual banks — institutions that have no branches. You can't visit a teller and usually you have to use another bank's ATMs. Most of your dealings with the bank are online or by phone.

Lower Fees and Better Rates

Virtual banks offer better deals on checking accounts. That was the clear conclusion of Bankrate.com's latest checking study. The semiannual look at checking accounts across the U.S. showed that Internet banks clearly offered the best deals.

Bankrate.com analyst Greg McBride says, "... The list of attributes to the accounts offered by Internet banks is extensive — competitive yields, lower service fees and bounced-check fees than brick-and-mortar accounts, more modest thresholds needed to avoid fees and a predominant number of accounts that are free or lack monthly service charges."

Customers of virtual banks have to bear one major financial disadvantage: ATM surcharges.

Most brick-and-mortar banks don't charge their account holders for using the bank's own ATMs. Most banks levy these ATM surcharges. Since most virtual banks don't own ATMs, their customers have to pay surcharges.

Some virtual banks will reimburse you for a few surcharges, but other virtual banks make you pay all surcharges. If you're a frequent ATM user, it might be cheaper to keep an account at a brick-and-mortar bank.

More Convenient Than You Think

Brick-and-mortar and clicks-and-mortar banks offer more convenience. It's nice to be able to drop in on a teller during your lunch break, or to complain to a branch manger when the bank makes a mistake. You can't do those things with an online bank. And with many online banks, you can't make a deposit at an ATM.

It's harder to make deposits at online banks. With most, you have to mail deposits or transfer money electronically from another account. Even if you set up direct deposit for your paychecks, you still get the occasional check, whether it's a gift, a payment at a garage sale, or a product rebate.

A few online banks have attacked this problem aggressively. Juniper Bank, for example, lets you drop off noncash deposits at Mail Boxes etc. locations, and so does National Interbank.

Other banks make arrangements with regional ATM networks to allow account holders to make deposits at the machines. Juniper, NetBank and First Internet Bank of Indiana are among the online banks that take deposits at ATMs, but the banks cover some areas better than others.

Protecting Yourself Online

Accounts that are insured by the Federal Deposit Insurance Corp. are covered regardless of whether the bank is virtual, clicks-and-mortar, or brick-and-mortar. Your money, up to $100,000, is safe at an FDIC-insured institution.

As always, you should zealously guard the user name and password of any online accounts. That's the most important security step. Banks have a pretty good track record when it comes to security.

All banks, whether they are virtual or not, have to abide by federal privacy laws and regulations. The rules are not particularly strong. Most financial institutions will share information about you with corporate affiliates and outside marketers unless you deny permission. A few have "opt-in" policies, meaning they won't share your information unless you give permission.

Supplementary Vocabulary

bank account	银行账户
bank book	银行存折
bank clerk	银行职员
bank deposit	银行存款
bank draft	银行汇票
banker	银行家
bank holiday	银行假日
bank paper	银行票据
bank rate	银行利率
open account	开立账户

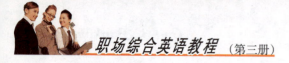

minimum deposit	最低存款额
bank charge	银行收费
service charge	手续费
interest	利息
interest rate	利率
current account/current deposit	活期存款账户
fixed account/fixed deposit	定期存款账户
current/fixed deposit account	活期/定期存款账户
deposit receipt	存款收据
a checking account	支票账户
a savings account	储蓄账户
certificate of deposit	存单
account balance	账户余额
to fill in the receipt in duplicate	一式两份填写这张收据
teller/cashier	出纳
passbook	存折
joint account	联名账户
separate account	单独账户
bill/note	钞票,纸币
cash a check	兑换支票
cash a money order	兑现汇款单
cash the balance of a traveler's letter of credit	兑现旅行信用证的余额
a ten-dollar bill	一张十美元的钞票
a five-pound note	五英镑的纸币
exchange	兑换,交换
exchange rate	兑换率
currency	货币
Foreign Currency Exchange	外币兑换业务
money exchange counter	兑换柜台
overdraft	透支
to honor a check	承兑支票
to dishonor a check	拒付支票
insufficient funds	资金不足

Unit 4

Supermarket

Learning Objectives:

You are able to:

☞ Know how to do shopping and choose necessities in the supermarket

☞ Know some familiar words and expressions used in the supermarket.

☞ Negotiate with assistants about the prices of items and the methods of payment

☞ Complain and settle a claim

Language Focus

ketchup	番茄酱	liquor store	售酒的商店
crisp	薯片	customer services	顾客服务处
beverage	饮料	massive stock	大量库存
priority	优先权	condiment	调味品
guarantee	保证	discount	折扣
receipt	收据	rollback	特惠
retain	保留	shopping cart	购物手推车
organic	有机的	kindly reminder	温馨提示
aisle	走廊,过道	always low price	天天低价
refund	退款		

Part I Listening and Speaking

Task 1   Listening Practice

Dialogue 1   Shopping in the supermarket

Directions: Now you will hear a conversation. Listen carefully and choose the best answer from the four choices.

1. Where does the conversation take place?
   A) in the street shop   B) in the supermarket
   C) in the liquor store   D) in the department stores
2. How to identify the organic vegetables?
   A) They look quite new and fresh. B) They are classified in a specific area.
   C) They are marked with blue label. D) The assistants will lead you to the aisle.
3. What is soy sauce?
   A) a kind of foods   B) a kind of dressings
   C) a kind of furniture   D) a kind of cosmetics
4. Did they want to drive up?
   A) They used the service, for the bags are too heavy.
   B) They used the service, for they are going to the magazine rack.
   C) They didn't use the service, for their car was not parked far away.
   D) They didn't use the service, for it should be paid.

Exercise 2   Promotions in the supermarket

Directions: Now you will hear a conversation. You are required to put in the missing information.

   Helen came to the supermarket to buy some _____, there happened to be a promotion for the item, so the final price is _____. When she checked out, the cashier asks her, did her want _____, she paid the bill by _____, and enter the _____.

Exercise 3   Shopping in the U.S.A

Directions: Now you will hear a short passage. You are required to put in the missing information

   When making a _____ in the United States, you should be _____ that, in most cases, the price on the _____ is not the price you pay. You will have to pay tax also. Usually the tax is between five and ten percent of the price on the label. Also, in buying clothes including shoes, you should know that the sizes are _____ differently in the U.S from the way they are measured in China where we use the metric system. In these cases, you can always ask the _____ for help.

• Unit 4 Supermarket •

Exercise 4 How to get your money's worth

Directions: Now you will hear a short dialogue. Listen carefully and decide whether the following statements are true or false.

_____ 1. Visitors often get confused by various kinds of sales in the U.S.
_____ 2. The best way to get your money's worth is to buy the cheapest items in the stores.
_____ 3. Goods bought on sales can be exchanged.
_____ 4. The advertisement provides all kinds of prices, so that you can make a comparison between these items.

Task 2 Oral Practice

Exercise 1

Directions: Here are some expressions often appeared in the supermarket, try to figure out the Chinese meaning of them.

1. Customer care is our top priority.
2. Easy to use and great value too.
3. Offer is subject to availability.
4. Please retain this receipt as proof of your purchase and your guarantee.
5. As many repairs as you need, free of charge.
6. Fill in your selection here and take to a pay point.

Exercise 2

Directions: Work in groups. Try to make a dialogue with your partner about shopping in the supermarket, you can follow the procedure in the below.

You come to a supermarket to buy toothbrushes, the assistant introduces different kinds of toothbrushes for you.

> * You make a shopping list
> * Come to the supermarket and pick up the things you want to buy
> * Look at the label to find the aisle you want to go
> * Put the things into the trolley
> * Check out at the checkout counter
> * You can choose to pay in cash or by card

Part II Reading

Text A

Before Reading:
1. Do you have experience in shopping in TESCO? How does it feel?
2. Do you hold some club cards or coupons of supermarket?

TESCO

If an anthropologist wanted to know what Britain was like, he would do well to take his notebook to Tesco. That's partly because it sells a third of Britain's groceries. But it is also because Tesco's customers are made up of the wealthy, middling and poor in just the same proportions as shoppers in the country as a whole. Tesco has become big by being like Britain.

At the beginning of the 1990s Tesco occupied a smaller, relatively down-market slot. In a country where people still saw class in where others shopped, nice upper-middle-class mothers went to J. Sainsbury or Waitrose. Since then, Tesco has prospered by conquering the centre ground. The store that was once best known for being cheap now stocks expensive beef fillets in elaborately concocted sauces.

It has been a fabulously successful strategy. Tesco is the biggest retailer in Britain, where it employs more than 250,000. The third-largest retailer in the world, it made an underlying pre-tax profit of more than £2 billion ($3.5 billion) last year on sales of £37 billion. It is still growing at home, but is also expanding abroad, with investments in Poland, Thailand, South Korea, Ireland and Hungary. So what changed?

Part of the answer is Britain itself. As Britons became more middle-class, Tesco followed them up-market. And it has made better use than its rivals of technology to find out exactly what they like.

Tesco is always hungry for new data: it recently called University College London's geography department to discuss new ways to slice up statistics. But most of its information comes from the Tesco Club card, a customer-loyalty scheme that allows Tesco to record what people are buying. Shoppers each buying 20 items a week would generate more than 12 billion pieces of data each year. Tesco can then explore links between purchases of different items—Turkey Twizzlers and claret, say—and market them in the store accordingly. "We believe we have one of the largest databases anywhere in the world," says Martin Hayward of Dunnhumby, the company that handles it for Tesco.

This knowledge allows Tesco to do two things. First, it can lavish attention on customers by giving them discounts on things that they buy routinely. Each cardholder gets a letter at the end of each quarter containing vouchers worth 1% of what they have spent. But they also get coupons that entitle them to discounts on products that Tesco's database, working much like the software that powers Amazon.com, suggests they might like. Last quarter, the store sent out 6m versions of this letter, each offering slightly different discounts.

Second, Tesco can adjust its shelves to suit the profile of the local area, or even the time of day. Tesco in Brixton, an area of south London settled by immigrants from the Caribbean, sells plantains, a kind of savory banana that can also be found for sale on market stalls outside. Tesco stores in central London do not, but are instead designed around selling sandwiches to office workers at lunchtime and then ready-meals to them in the evening. The aim is to combine the local knowledge of the village shop with a multinational's economies of scale in buying and logistics.

But, thanks to its size, Tesco is also changing the country that Sir Terry Leahy, its chief executive, says it mirrors. Some of these changes are small. The dust jacket of a book that was to be sold in-store was recently altered because a Tesco buyer did not like it. Others are more fundamental. Before the Club card came along, the largest panels that suppliers could use consisted of around 20,000 people. But suppliers can now pay for access to the database and many just rely on Tesco. This dependence means there is an information loop, in which a product is developed and perfected according to the tics of the Tesco customers—who will determine its success.

New Words

anthropologist	/ˌænθrəˈpɒlədʒist/	n.	人类学家
grocery	/ˈɡrəʊs(ə)ri/	n.	食品杂货店;食品杂货业
proportion	/prəˈpɔːʃ(ə)n/	n.	比,比率
slot	/slɒt/	n.	位置;狭槽,
prosper	/ˈprɒspə/	v.	繁盛,成功
fillet	/ˈfilit/	n.	肉片,鱼片
elaborately	/iˈlæb(ə)rətli/	adv.	苦心经营地,精巧地;精心
concoct	/kənˈkɒkt/	v.	调制;捏造,图谋,策划
fabulously	/ˈfæbjʊləsli/	adv.	难以置信地,惊人地
strategy	/ˈstrætidʒi/	n.	策略,战略,战略学
retailer	/ˈriːteilə(r)/	n.	零售商,零售店
claret	/ˈklærət/	n.	红葡萄酒;深红色
lavish	/ˈlæviʃ/	adj.	过分慷慨的;非常浪费的
routinely	/ruːˈtiːnli/	adv.	例行公事地;常规地
voucher	/ˈvaʊtʃə/	n.	证件;凭证;收据;证人
coupon	/ˈkuːpɒn/	n.	优惠券;息票,通票

immigrant	/ˈimigr(ə)nt/	n.	移民,侨民;从异地移入的动物
plantain	/ˈplantin, -tein/	n.	车前草
savory	/ˈseiv(ə)ri/	n.	(烹调用的)香薄荷
logistic	/ləˈdʒistik/	adj.	逻辑的
loop	/luːp/	n.	圈,环

Phrases and Expressions

| slice up | 划分 |

Exercises

I. Answer the following questions according to the passage.

1. If the anthropologist wants to know Britain, why the author says he can go to Tesco?

2. What does "J. Sainsbury or Waitrose" refer to in the passage?

3. What's the function of "Tesco Clubcard"?

4. What kinds of methods does Tesco use to attract customers?

5. Why does Tesco often adjust its shelves?

II. Fill in the blanks with the proper words and expressions given below, changing the form if necessary.

| grocery | lavish | entitle to | conquer | alter |
| slice up | proportion | combine | investment | adjust to |

1. They lived a very _____ lifestyle.
2. Some countries may be defeated but can never be _____.
3. He was employed at the local _____ store as a delivery boy.
4. Take out the seeds before you _____ the fruit.
5. Foreigners take some time to _____ our way of life.
6. They have never _____ their programmers by a single day.
7. The _____ of imports to exports is worrying the government.

8. Some films _____ education with recreation.
9. Your qualifications _____ you _____ a higher salary.
10. Lack of confidence is the biggest barrier to _____ in the region.

III. Translate the following sentences into Chinese.
1. If an anthropologist wanted to know what Britain was like, he would do well to take his notebook to Tesco.
2. And it has made better use than its rivals of technology to find out exactly what they like.
3. But most of its information comes from the Tesco Clubcard, a customer-loyalty scheme that allows Tesco to record what people are buying.
4. Each cardholder gets a letter at the end of each quarter containing vouchers worth 1% of what they have spent.

IV. Translate the following sentences into English.
1. 这项建议引起众多的关注。(*generate*)
2. 自从他的生意兴隆以来,他们一直过着优越的生活。(*prosper*)
3. 希望我们能想出最佳的宣传策略。(*strategy*)
4. 无论如何只要支付现金,就必须要有一张凭据或收据。(*voucher*)
5. 移民故事一直是小说中常见的主题。(*immigrant*)

Text B

Before Reading:
1. Have you ever done shopping in some department store?
2. Can you tell us your experience about shopping?

The Department Store

One of the features of large cities is the number of big department stores, most of which are to be found in or near the central area. They are vast buildings many stories high, where you can buy almost anything you need, from a box of toothpicks to a suite of furniture.

Most of them are very modern and are equipped with convenient elevators and escalators, and have well-planned air-conditioning and ventilation. You can spend hours wandering around in one of these department stores, and you will probably lose your way while you are doing so, in spite of many signs pointing the way to the elevators and exits. If you have been in one of the stores so long that you feel hungry, you and your friends will not need to leave the building, for nearly all the big stores have cafes, snack bars or restaurants in them. After a meal, you can inspect the goods on sale at your leisure, and you will not be pestered to buy anything, though occasionally an assistant may ask you whether he or she can be of help to you.

Another feature of people's shopping life is the chain-store, in which prices are lower than in the big store, and a wide variety of goods are offered, such as foodstuffs, household goods, clothing and stationery. The goods are displayed on open shelves and counters, and it is a regrettable fact that some shopliftings go on sometimes, in spite of the vigilance of the store security guards.

A lot of the food stores now operate on the "serve-yourself" system: you go in, pick up a basket or a cart, walk round the shop and choose what you need. At the exit there are a number of counters where you pay for all your purchase together. This system cuts down the firm's expenses, for fewer assistants are required. It is the method used in the great and still growing number of supermarkets. Large self-service stores chiefly concerned with the sale of foodstuffs, but increasingly with other types of goods as well.

New Words

toothpicks	/tuːθpiks/	n.	牙签
suite	/swiːt/	n.	套件；一套，一副
elevator	/ˈeliveitə/	n.	电梯；升降机（美）
escalator	/ˈeskəleitə/	n.	自动扶梯
ventilation	/ventiˈleiʃ(ə)n/	n.	空气流通；通风设备
wander	/ˈwɒndə/	v.	漫步，漫游
snack	/snak/	n.	快餐，点心；加餐
inspect	/inˈspekt/	v.	检查，检验；视察
pester	/ˈpestə/	v.	使烦恼；使为难；纠缠
occasionally	/əˈkeiʒ(ə)n(ə)li/	adv.	偶尔，间或
display	/diˈsplei/	v.	显示；陈列
regrettable	/riˈgretəb(ə)l/	adj.	令人遗憾的；可惜的
shoplifting	/ˈʃɒpliftiŋ/	n.	商店行窃
vigilance	/ˈvidʒil(ə)ns/	n.	警觉；警惕
cart	/kɑːt/	n.	运货马车，手推车
counter	/ˈkaʊntə/	n.	柜台

Exercises

I. Read the above passage carefully and decide whether the following statements are true or false.

____ 1. You can get almost anything in the department store.

____ 2. If you don't buy something in the store, you will be bothered by some assistants.
____ 3. If you are hungry you can get some snacks in the department store.
____ 4. There are some thieves in the chain-store, though many guards keep watch on the goods.
____ 5. If you go to a shop operate on the "serve-yourself" system, you can check out by yourself.

II. Fill in the blanks with the proper words and expressions given below, changing the form if necessary.

| wander | inspect | occasionally | display | purchase |
| pester | shoplift | regrettable | counter | concern with |

1. If she carries on _____, she'll end up in jail
2. I asked the woman behind the _____, if they had any postcards.
3. The details of today's flights are _____ on the monitor
4. Most equipment on the dairy farm was _____ with the worker's own earnings
5. We could not prove he was _____ the crime, so we had to release him.
6. They perceived a stranger _____ in the garden.
7. I thought she'd stop _____ me, but it only seemed to make her worse.
8. It is highly _____ that the minister cannot be here in person.
9. He went on talking, _____ wiping at his face with a towel.
10. Two policemen held up a truck so as to _____ the driver's license.

III. Pay attention to different parts of speech and select the appropriate word to fill in the blank.

1. object, objective, objection
   a. He has a strong _____ to getting up so early.
   b. A stationary _____ is easy to be aimed at.
   c. She gives an _____ report of what has happened.
2. origin, original, originality
   a. His Nobel Prize is a tribute to the _____ of his research.
   b. The room still has many of its _____ features.
   c. Earthquakes are grouped according to their _____, into three classes.
3. respective, respectable, respectful
   a. He receives guests with a _____ attitude.
   b. They went into their _____ bedrooms to pack.
   c. His savings were just enough to pay for a _____ funeral.
4. occasion, occasional, occasionally
   a. He went on talking, _____ wiping at his face with a towel.
   b. Her dress was too showy for such a formal _____.
   c. The weather was good except for an _____ shower.

5. regret, regrettable, regretful
   a. Mother was most _____ when she saw the remains of the meal.
   b. The Prime Minister expressed her _____ at the failure of the talks.
   c. It's _____ that Bob did not follow your instructions.

IV. Class Work

Nowadays "shopping mall" become prosperous, discuss the influences "shopping mall" brings to our lives.

Part III Writing

Complaints and Claims

Component of letters of complaints

Regret the need to complain

Give details to explain what is wrong

State your reasons for being dissatisfied and ask for an explanation

Refer to the inconvenient it caused

Suggest how the matter should be put right

Example

Letters of complaints

Oct 28, 2012

Dear manager,

　　I am writing to show my great anger about the bad service I encountered in your department store last Sunday. That saleswoman (No.198) was by no means patient enough to answer my questions about products. She was so eagerly talking with her friend that she just turned a deaf ear to my questions. I felt disappointed that such bad service should have happened in a so-call five-star department store.

　　I hope you do something to stop such things happening any more, just to save your store's fame.

　Yours sincerely
　　May Bates

Unit 4 Supermarket

Component of letters of claims

> Inform the receiver of the details related to the goods to be claimed
> Make clear what your claim is
> Request the action: a replacement, repair or refund

Example

> **Claims of damage of goods**
>
> Dear sir,
>
> Our order NO.172
>
> The glassware you supplies to our order of 3rd July was delivered by shipping company this morning. The 160 cartons contains the goods appear to be in perfect condition, but when I unpacked them with great care, I regret to report that 10 cartons of glassware had been badly cracked.
>
> We trust that you can understand that we expect the compensation for our damaged goods.
>
> Yours faithfully
>   John Thomas

Exercise:

Suppose that you ordered a refrigerator but later found a worrying problem. Write a letter of complaint to describe the matter and require the settlement.

Part IV Cultural Express

Factory Outlets

If you plan on going outlet shopping, spend some time online before you head out. Visiting the websites of the outlets you are interested in can save you big. Some outlet centers are generous. You can register for their free VIP club online and get access to dozens of online coupons as well as print a special VIP coupon book voucher to show at the information desk to get even more coupons. Even with the less generous outlets, you can still find some printable coupons to use. Remember to print out multiple copies of each one since sometimes things only apply to a single item.

If you miss those online discounts, do not worry. The outlet centers always have coupons at the information center. But you have to either have an AAA membership or a VIP pass to get the coupons. If you don't have either of them, you can still buy the coupon book with a couple of dollars. Before you purchase, you can ask to see the coupon book to see if it is worth the fee.

There are two kinds of outlets stores: those that are just last season retail stores with a slight markdown and those that are real outlets, where things are deeply discounted for quick sale. If you are serious bargain hunter, look for things that are really good deals, not 20% off retail price. To achieve that, you can do a little comparison shopping throughout the outlet center before buying. Most shops will hold items for their costumers if requested. By doing so, you can gain more time and avoid impulsive shopping.

Most factory outlets carry overstocks of the same first grade merchandise you find in the parent store at considerably reduced prices. Along with the overstocks, there are even more budget-friendly options on irregulars and factory seconds. What are "factory seconds" and 'irregulars"? Factory seconds and irregulars are not necessarily faulty or even of lessened quality, but rather a piece of merchandise with a minor problem (typically cosmetic and easily reparable) that prevent it from passing the quality checks in the inspection process, as a result, preventing it from being shipped to the parent store counterpart, apparel may contain irregular or mis-marked size tags or hanging threads that a quick snip can get it fixed in no time. Pay special attention to apparel items, and always try them on before you take them home. Even if you are allowed to return, replace or refund what you buy, you still need to keep it on mind if you are on vacation, that it might be a long trip to return or exchange an item after you make the purchase. So, look everything over carefully and do not get carried away by the fun and excitement of bargain hunting.

Unit 4　Supermarket

Questions:
1. How many kinds of outlet stores introduced in the passage?
2. What are "factory seconds" and 'irregulars"?

Supplementary Vocabulary

frozen food	冷冻食品
dairy products	乳制品
pet food	宠物食品
confectionery	糖业类
toiletries	厕所用品
cereals	谷类食品
poultry	家禽类
pickle	各式腌菜
outlet	专营店，直销店
bridge line	高端品牌的低端产品
closeout	清仓产品
damaged	问题产品
factory direct	厂家直销
off-price retailer	折扣零售商
out of season	过季商品
overrun	超额产品
factory second	厂家次货

Unit 5

Enterprise

Learning Objectives:
You are able to:
☞ Learn how to get the information about other companies
☞ Use the proper expressions to introduce your own company
☞ Be familiar with the office manners
☞ Write a company profile

Language Focus

joint venture　合资企业
contract　合同，契约
company image　公司形象
interpersonal skills　人际交往能力
administrative skills　行政管理能力
sales manager　销售经理
office clerk　办公室文员
senior consultant　专业顾问
consulting director　咨询总监
security custody clerk　安保人员
phone operator　电话接线员
professional staff　专业人员
branch manager　部门经理
marketing supervisor　市场部主管
regional sales representative　区域销售代表
market analyst /research analyst　市场分析师
general manager　总经理（president）
Head office　总部

Branch office　分公司
Business office　营业部
Advertising department　广告部
Planning department　企划部
Personnel resources department
　人力资源部
Sales department　销售部
Product development department
　产品研发部
Public relations department
　公关部
Marketing department　营销部
Financial department　财务部
Purchasing / Procurement department
　采购部
After-sale service department
　售后服务部
Quality control department
　质检部
Technology department　技术部

• Unit 5   Enterprise •

Part I   Listening and Speaking

Task 1   Listening Practice

Exercise 1   Job interview

Directions: Now you will hear a short dialogue. Listen carefully and choose the best answer from the four choices.

1. The interviewee graduates from _____.
   A. Nanjing Normal University
   B. Nanjing University
   C. Nanjing University of Science & Technology
2. The interviewee is excellent in _____.
   A. spoken English   B. written English   C. reading English
3. The interviewee looking for a position in the department of _____.
   A. personnel   B. marketing   C. software engineering
4. The interviewee's salary expectation is _____.
   A. 3000   B. 3000 to 5000   C. 5000

Exercise 2   First Day at Work

Directions: Now you will hear a conversation. You are required to put in the missing information.

M: Welcome aboard!
W: Thank you. I'm ____1____ to be working here, Mr. Buchwald. It's a pleasure to meet you again.
M: Call me Buck, will you? My name is Reginald Buchwald, but everybody call me Buck. It's easier.
W: I would hesitate to call you anything but Mr. Buchwald. Isn't it rather disrespectful to make a nickname out of the ____2____?
M: Well, President Eisenhower was known as Ike. Everybody in this company all the way up and down the line is called by his first name. It's been ____3____ ever since the company was small. And don't worry about ____4____. OK?
W: I'll try.
M: Good. But when there are outsiders, like business people from other companies, it might be good practice to ____5____ your higher-ups as Mr., Ms., or whatever is appropriate. To the outside world, our custom may be interpreted as a sign of flippancy or lax discipline. Get it?
W: Yes, sir.

M (laughing): And don't sir me either. Now I'll show you your private office... Now, this is our office block. We have all the administrative departments in it. Our office is on the third floor.

W: Shall I meet my colleagues?

M: Sure, come with me.

Exercise 3   Establishing business relations

Directions: Now you will hear a conversation. You are required to put in the missing information.

Amanda: Good morning. My name is Amanda Beard. I'm from Australia.

Kathy: I'm pleased to meet you, miss. Beard. My name is Kathy Eden, the representative of Green Textile Import and Export Corporation.

Amanda: Pleased to meet you too, Ms. Eden. I travel a lot every year ____1____, but this is my first visit to your country. I must say I have been much impressed by your friendly people.

Kathy: Thank you for saying so. Have you seen the exhibition halls? There are most of our products ____2____.

Amanda: Oh, yes. I had a look yesterday. I found some of the exhibits to be ____3____ in quality and ____4____ in design. I've got some idea of your exports. I'm interested in your silk blouses.

Kathy: Our silk is known for its good quality. It is one of our traditional exports. Silk blouses are brightly colored and beautifully designed.

Amanda: That sounds interesting. I'll send a fax home. As soon as I receive a definite answer, I'll make a specific inquiry.

Kathy: We'll then ____5____ as soon as possible. I hope a lot of business will be conducted between us.

Amanda: So do I.

Exercise 4

Directions: Now you will hear a short passage. Listen carefully and decide whether the following statements are true or false.

_____ 1. The company has a history of about 100 years.

_____ 2. The company mainly produce electronic goods.

_____ 3. The company have offices in South America with about 1 000 employees.

_____ 4. We need reliable agents to market our products at home.

• Unit 5 Enterprise •

Task 2 Oral Practice

Directions: Work in pairs. Each can choose to be role A or Role B, and make an introduction of your company, including company profile, employees, turnover, plan and your job duties.

> Position: Technical Director. Mata Shoes
> Duties: responsible for quality control of products
>   works with the Design Department to create new products
> Company profile: one of the biggest shoe manufactures in Brazil
>   manufactures shoes under the brand name "Daniela"
> Employees: 20 000
> Turnover last year: USD 550 million
> Plan: to enter new markets next year

Task 3 Class Work

Now you see a profile of a company.

> Location: Eastern suburb of Guangzhou
> Established: 1989
> Headquarters: Los Angeles, USA
> Number of employees: 2,509
> Main products: Electronic products, including mobile phones, DVD players, TV sets
>   and hi-fi equipment
> Turnover last year: US$ 8,000,000,000
> Turnover this year: US$ 950,000,000

Exercise:
Suppose you are the Managing Director of the company. A reporter comes to interview you about your company. Be prepared to answer his or her questions.

Part II Reading

Text A

Before Reading:
1. What kinds of mobile phone do you want to buy? Which operating system will you choose?
2. Do you know who established the Apple Company? How much do you know about him?

Introduction of Apple Inc.

Company profile

Apple Inc. (formerly Apple Computer, Inc.) is an American multinational corporation that designs and sells consumer electronics, computer software, and personal computers. The company's best-known hardware products are the Macintosh line of computers, the iPod, the iPhone and the iPad (Apple calls its computers Macintoshes or Macs, and it calls its laptops MacBooks. Their popular line of mobile music players are called iPods and a smart phone they have released is called the iPhone.). Its software includes the OSX and iOS operating system; the iTunes media browser; and the iLife and iWork creativity and production suites. Apple is the world's third-largest mobile phone maker after Samsung and Nokia. Established on April 1, 1976 in Cupertino, California, and incorporated January 3, 1977, the company was named Apple Computer, Inc. for its first 30 years. The word "Computer" was removed from its name on January 9, 2007, as its traditional focus on personal computers shifted towards consumer electronics.

Current products

1. iPad

On January 27, 2010, Apple introduced their much-anticipated media tablet, the iPad running a modified version of iOS.

2. iPod

The current iPod family, featuring the iPod Shuffle, iPod Nano, iPod Classic, and iPod Touch

3. iPhone

On October 4, 2011, Apple unveiled the iPhone 4S, which was released in the United States, Canada, Australia, United Kingdom, France, Germany, and Japan on October 14, 2011, with other countries set to follow later in the year. Apple sold two million iPhone's in the first twenty four hours of pre ordering.

4. Apple TV

At the 2007 Macworld conference, Jobs demonstrated the Apple TV, (previously known as the iTV), a set-top video device intended to bridge the sale of content from iTunes with high-definition televisions.

Name and Logos

According to Steve Jobs, Apple was so named because Jobs was coming back from an apple farm, and he was on a fruitarian diet. He thought the name was "fun, spirited and not intimidating".

 The original logo with Isaac Newton under an apple tree

 The rainbow "bitten" logo, used from late 1976 to 1998

 The monochrome logo, used since 1998

Fortune magazine named Apple the most admired company in the United States in 2008, and in the world from 2008 to 2012.

● Unit 5　Enterprise ●

New Words

multinational	/mʌltɪˈnæʃ(ə)n(ə)l/	adj.	多国的;跨国的
laptop	/ˈlaptɒp/	n.	便携式电脑
release	/rɪˈliːs/	v.	释放;放开;发布;发行
establish	/ɪˈstablɪʃ, ɛ-/	v.	建立,创建;确立或使安全
remove	/rɪˈmuːv/	v.	去除;脱掉,拿下
anticipate	/anˈtɪsɪpeɪt/	v.	预感;预见;预料;先于……行动
feature	/ˈfiːtʃə/	v.	使有特色;起主要作用;作重要角色
unveil	/ʌnˈveɪl/	v.	揭去……的面罩;使公之于众;揭露
demonstrate	/ˈdɛmənstreɪt/	v.	证明,证实;显示,展示;演示,说明
bridge	/brɪdʒ/	v.	在……建桥,架桥于……之上
diet	/ˈdʌɪət/	n.	日常饮食;规定饮食
intimidate	/ɪnˈtɪmɪdeɪt/	v.	恐吓,威胁

Phrases and Expressions

smart phone	智能手机
much-anticipated media tablet	备受期待的平板电脑

Proper Names

Fortune magazine	《财富》杂志

Exercises

I. Answer the following questions according to the passage.

1. What does Apple Inc. design and sell?

　

2. What is Apple Inc.'s best known hardware products?

　

3. When was the company established?

　

4. What is Apple Inc.'s original name?

5. And When did the company begin to use the name Apple Inc. and why?

II. Fill in the blanks with the proper words and expressions given below, changing the form if necessary.

| release | establish | remove | feature |
| demonstrate | bridge | unveil | intimidate |

1. At least three bullets were _____ from his wounds,
2. Our latest smart phone is _____ by multi-functions
3. Figures _____ yesterday show retail sales were down in March.
4. The School was _____ in 1989 by an Italian professor.
5. A style consultant will _____ how to dress to impress.
6. It is unlikely that the two sides will be able to _____ their differences
7. The Princess _____ a plaque.
8. The forts are designed to _____ the nationalist population.

III. Translate the following sentences into Chinese.

1. The word "Computer" was removed from its name on January 9, 2007, as its traditional focus on personal computers shifted towards consumer electronics.
2. Apple was so named because Jobs was coming back from an apple farm, and he was on a fruitarian diet. He thought the name was "fun, spirited and not intimidating".
3. Fortune magazine named Apple the most admired company in the United States in 2008, and in the world from 2008 to 2012.
4. On January 27, 2010, Apple introduced their much-anticipated media tablet, the iPad running a modified version of iOS.

IV. Translate the following sentences into English.
1. 苹果公司是从事设计和销售电子消费品、电脑软件和个人电脑的跨国公司。
2. 苹果公司是世界上第三大手机生产商,仅次于三星和诺基亚。
3. 公司最著名的的计算机产品是电脑、音乐播放器、手机和平板电脑。
4. 在首个24小时预订中,苹果共售出200万部iPhone。

Text B

Before Reading:
Work in groups and discuss the office etiquettes you know.

How to Face Your First Day Like a Pro

You rocked the résumé, nailed the interview, and landed the job. Congratulations! Now it's time to get to work. Your first day on the job can feel both exciting and nerve-wracking, so here's how to handle the first-day jitters like a pro and leave a lasting impression on your new coworkers.

• **Show up on time:** Today is not the day to try a new coffee shop or take a shortcut to work. Being on time is always important, but today especially. Before your first day, ask your manager what time you should arrive, and show up at precisely that time — not too early and certainly not late. Also, try mapping out or even traveling your route beforehand, that way you will know exactly where to go and how long it will take. Yes, there is more!

• **Play the name game:** On your first day, you will be introduced to several new faces, which can often seem overwhelming. To ensure you don't forget the names of important people, ask for a seating chart, and use these tactics to remember names.

• **Overdress:** No, you don't have to show up in a ball gown, but do look the part. Even if you are unsure of the office dress code and environment (casual or corporate), it's hard to go wrong with chic and simple business attire, like a fitted blazer. Don't be afraid to add a touch of personal style, as well.

• **Bring a notebook:** Just like your high-school days, bring a notebook and don't let it leave your side! You will be introduced to so much new information, tricks, and tips that will be important to remember beyond your first day. Plus, jotting down notes will help you to better remember these tips in the long run.

• **Ask questions:** Don't be afraid to ask more about a topic or to address any concerns you may have, even if the answer is simple. Your coworkers will be more than understanding and willing to help! Plus, asking smart questions shows you are interested and engaged.

• **Observe, observe, observe:** Soak it all in! Watching is the best way to learn and get a feel for your new job and office environment.

Your first day is exciting, but remember to be yourself and enjoy the moment. Soon enough, that first day will feel like ages ago.

New Words

pro	/prəʊ/	n.	赞成者；赞成的意见；赞成票，投赞成票者
jitter	/ˈdʒɪtə/	n.	神经过敏；极度紧张；激动(jitter 的复数)
tactic	/ˈtæktɪk/	n.	手段；策略；战术；战略
attire	/əˈtaɪə/	n.	服装，衣服
blazer	/ˈbleɪzə/	n.	（法兰绒的）运动上衣
engaged	/ɪnˈgeɪdʒd/	adj.	正忙着的，忙碌的

Phrases and Expressions

leave a(n) ... impression on/upon	给……留下……印象
show up	出现露面
jot down	草草记下，匆匆记下
in the long run	从长远来看

Exercises

I. Read the above passage carefully and then decide whether the following statements are true or false.

____ 1. It's necessary to ask your manager what time you should arrive.
____ 2. On the first day you won't meet many new faces.
____ 3. A notebook is needed to help you to better remember the names of important people.
____ 4. Your coworkers are willing to answer your questions.
____ 5. The best way to learn and get a feel for your new job is observing and practicing.

II. Fill in the blanks with the proper words and expressions given below, changing the form if necessary.

precisely	engaged	jitter	impression
on time	ensure	jot down	in the long run

1. Of course, they would be nervous with new-job _____.
2. He was eager to share his _____ and opinions on my writings.
3. We should pay our bills _____.
4. The incident has prompted police to warn parents to _____ the safety of children in cars.

70

5. When you've found the answers, _____ them _____.
6. The project will both use a renewable source of power as well as save the university money _____.
7. Its leaders are actively _____ right now looking for a solution.
8. I can identify the moment I fell out of love with India quite _____.

III. **Pay attention to different parts of speech and select the appropriate word to fill in the blank.**

1. impress, impression, impressive
   a. I was very _____ by her performance.
   b. This cinema is so _____ that we can't help crying.
   c. She made a good _____ on his mother.
2. tactical, tactic
   a. When he saw a new _____, he would write it down in his notebook.
   b. It's just a _____ device to get over a split in their own Party
3. engage, engaged, engagement
   a. I can't see you on Monday because I have a previous _____.
   b. Please wait a minute, he is _____ just now.
   c. I have no time to _____ in the debate.
4. interview (v.), interview(n.), interviewee
   a. Don't be late for your job _____.
   b. He was among the three candidates _____ for the job.
   c. The success depends on good rapport between interviewer and _____.
5. precisely, precise
   a. Can you give a more _____ definition of the word?
   b. But it is _____ because we do not do anything that we have not the money.

IV. **Class Work**

Work with your partner and try to repeat the main idea of the passage.

A Company Profile

The company profile is used to introduce a business organization as a whole. Alternatively, business organizations may choose to put the information in printed media to make their message known to their clients and the general public.

Company profile usually introduces a business organization as a whole in these respects: history, major business scope, ranges of products, market, business contacts, strategic objectives, sales volume, etc..

There are three parts in a company profile:

1. Introduction: It usually comes straight to the point. And It mainly introduces the business nature, history, location and reputation of the company.

2. Body: In this part, a company is introduced in these respects: business scope, equipments, ranges of products, market, business contacts, strategic objectives, sales volume, etc.

3. Close: There is the last paragraph, even one sentence of the company profile. It is to express the goodwill and hope. Sometimes, this part can be omitted.

Sample

> Haier refrigerator and washing machine are among the first group of Chinese World Famous Brand products awarded by the General Administration of Quality Supervision, Inspection and Quarantine of the P.R.C. in March 2008. Haier was selected as one of the "China's Top 10 Global Brands" by Financial Times for the second time. In June 2008, Haier ranked 13th and 1st among Chinese companies on the list of the world's "600 Most Reputable Companies", released by Forbes. In July 2008, Haier ranked first in terms of overall leadership among Chinese mainland companies in the Wall Street Journal Asia's annual survey of "Asia's 200 Most Admired Companies" for the fifth time. Haier has become an international brand, and its prestige is rising fast with its expansion into the international market.

Exercise:

Directions: Write a company profile according to the information given below.

我们公司成立于1986年，专业生产电子产品，集产品研发和生产于一体。我公司地处合肥市，交通便利。我公司所有产品采用国际质量标准，产品远销海外，享誉海内外众多市场。如果贵公司对我们任一款产品有意或有订单意向，欢迎随时联系我们。我们期待与全球客户携手合作，共创未来。

Part IV Cultural Express

Wal-Mart's Influence Grows

Wal-Mart's influence on the U.S. economy has reached levels not seen by a single company since the 19th-century rise of Standard Oil, economists and historians say.

Even if you don't shop at Wal-Mart,

the retail powerhouse increasingly is dictating your product choices — and what you pay — as its relentless price cutting helps keep inflation low.

Wal-Mart is the top seller of groceries, jewelry and photo processing. It is creating more of its own brands. Some, such as Ol' Roy dog food and Equate vitamins, quickly became the USA's top sellers. It is moving into banking, used car sales, travel and Internet access. It averages 100 million customers a week. That's 88.5 million more people than U.S. airlines fly in a week.

Anyone whose stocks rose in the late 1990s owes Wal-Mart, the world's biggest company. It alone accounted for as much as 25% of the U.S. productivity gains from 1995-1999, says consultant McKinsey & Co. Such gains drove corporate profits, thus stock prices. Wages in retailing, one of the biggest sources of new jobs in the 1990s and current decade, are also affected by Wal-Mart. With 1.3 million workers, it is the world's largest private employer. It employs one of every 123 U.S. workers and nearly one of every 20 retail employees.

"I joke we're all going to be working for Wal-Mart someday," says economist Mark Zandi of consultant Economy.com.

That may not be too far off.

Although Wal-Mart is hitting speed bumps because of growing labor challenges, employment lawsuits and higher costs, few doubt it will stop besting competitors as it expands. While other retailers such as Home Depot, tech giants such as Microsoft and manufacturers such as General Electric played big parts in the 1990s productivity gains, Wal-Mart, with its massive buying power and technology advantage, played the biggest role, economists say. As it grows, its influence, largely unknown to consumers, will continue to seep into more parts of the USA and the global economies.

"Everyone knows Wal-Mart," says Jim Hoopes, a business history professor at Babson College, "but nobody has a real sense of how big and how powerful it is."

Wal-Mart, responding to criticism over its growing influence, says it creates thousands of jobs a year and pays competitive wages and benefits. Its push for productivity is meant to keep prices low, benefiting its customers, says spokesman Tom Williams. "We're doing good, but we could do better," he says.

Few companies have moved so far so fast. Founded 40 years ago in rural Arkansas by Sam Walton, Wal-Mart has swelled to 4,300 stores in nine countries and annual revenue near $250 billion. Its computer network, a critical part of its success, rivals the Pentagon's.

It is now the biggest customer for many of the world's leading consumer-products companies, including Kraft, Gillette and Procter & Gamble. At P&G, Wal-Mart accounts for 17% of annual revenue, up from 10% just five years ago. That makes those companies more dependent on Wal-Mart's success, more vulnerable should it stumble and more likely to respond to Wal-Mart's requests for lower prices and product changes.

The chain's buying power is so immense that 450 suppliers have opened offices — many in the 1990s — near Wal-Mart headquarters in tiny Bentonville,

Ark. As many as 800 more such offices are expected in the next five years. Sales representatives want to be near Wal-Mart buyers to beat the competition, says Rich Davis, a local economic development official. "I've had them sit here and say, 'Look, if we're not here, our competitor will be,'" Davis says.

Supplementary Vocabulary

performance   业绩、表现
His performance this month has been less than satisfactory.
他这个月的业绩不是很令人满意。
Performance Evaluation   定期的员工个人评定
The performance evaluation test is a way of seeing how efficient a worker's performance is.
定期的员工个人评定是一种考察员工的工作有多高效的手段。
challenge   在外企的英文中它不当"挑战"讲而是"谴责、批评、指责"
His poor performance gave rise to the challenge from his boss.
他差劲的表现遭到了老板的批评。
presentation   做介绍(一般指打投影仪的那种汇报)
His presentation on the Earth Summit proves that we really need to pay more attention to the global environment.
他在地球峰会上的报告证实了我们的确要更加关注全球的环境。
quota   员工的(一年或半年的)任务量
Have you reached your predicted quota for this quarter?
你完成了本季度预期的任务量了吗?
solid   可靠的、稳妥的
Their partnership is solid as a rock. 他们的伙伴关系像岩石一样坚不可摧。
complicated   复杂的
English grammar is very complicated. 英语语法非常复杂。
vacation = leave 休假
It is my vacation soon, I think I'll go to Huang Shan to relax.
我马上就要休假了。我想我会去黄山放松一下。
follow up   把某件事情继续负责追究到底
Have you been following up on the news recently? 你有跟踪调查最近的新闻吗?
Foreign exchange swap center   外汇调剂中心
Formula Based Amortization   按公式计算的摊还方法
FASCO   外航服务公司   FIE   外商投资企业
GATS   服务贸易总协定   Regular subsidy to the family   定期抚恤金
The living subsides   生活费补贴   R/E=Retained Earning   未分配利润

Unit 6

Business Contact

Learning Objectives:

You are able to:

☞ Be familiar with the basic procedures of business contacts
☞ Know the process of a commercial transaction
☞ Conduct simple business conversation with the counterparts
☞ Write business memo

Language Focus

brochure	产品宣传册	showroom	展厅
representative	（销售）代表	import	进口
export	出口	line	产品种类
credit	信用	quote	报价

CIF (Cost, Insurance and Freight)
　　　　　成本加保险费加运费，包括从装运港至约定目的地港的通常运费和约定的保险费。

FOB(Free on Board)		warehouse	仓库
	离岸价	freight	运费
insurance	保险	forward agent	运送经纪人,运输行
clear	出口清关	delivery	运输
LC (letter of credit)		consignment	货物
	信用证	quotation	报价

Part I Listening and Speaking

Task 1 Listening Practice

Exercise 1   Establishing the business relationship

Directions: Now you will hear a short dialogue. Listen carefully and choose the best answer from the four choices.

1. Jack is the representative from _____.
    A. Sales department   B. Marketing department
    C. Production department   D. HR department
2. Jack got the information about the product from _____.
    A. TV commercial   B. newspaper advertisement
    C. brochure   D. other resources
3. Where is the showroom of the factory?
    A. half an hour's car ride from the factory
    B. in another city
    C. in the suburb
    D. not mentioned
4. When are they going to visit the showroom?
    A. three o'clock tomorrow morning   B. three o'clock tomorrow afternoon
    C. ten o'clock tomorrow morning   C. ten o'clock tomorrow afternoon

Exercise 2   Introducing the products and making further contact

Directions: Now you will hear a conversation. You are required to put in the missing information.

M: Good morning. My name is James Right. I'm from Australia. Here is my card.
W: Thank you. I'm glad to meet you, Mr. Right. My name is Li Hong, the representative of _____1_____.
M: Pleased to meet you too, Ms. Li. This is my first visit to your country and I have been much impressed by your friendly people.
W: Thank you for saying so. Have you visited our showroom? On display are most of our products, such as _____2_____, and garments.
M: Oh, yes. I went there this morning. I found some of the exhibits to be _____3_____. As I have mentioned in the last letter, I'm interested in your silk pajamas.
W: Our silk is known for its good quality. It is one of our traditional leading exports. Silk pajamas are beautifully designed and extremely comfortable to wear. They've met with _____4_____.
M: Some of them seem to be of the latest style. Now I've a feeling that we can do a lot of trade in this line. We wish to establish relations with you.

W: I am so glad to hear that and that is also what we have in mind.

M: Concerning _____5_____ , you may refer to Bank of Australia or inquiry agencies.

W: Thank you for your information. As you know, our corporation is a state-owned one. We always trade with foreign countries on the basis of equality and mutual benefit. I have no doubt that it will bring about closer ties between us.

M: That sounds interesting.

Exercise 3　Placing the order

Directions: Now you will hear a conversation. You are required to put in the missing information.

Mr. Williams: Good morning, Mr. Bai. Long time no see.

Mr. Bai: Good morning, Mr. Williams! You have a good shape, haven't you?

Mr. Williams: Yes, thank you. You look great, too. We've had your offer and are very much interested in it.

Mr. Bai: I am happy to hear that our specifications meet your requirements. I'm sure the prices quoted are ___1___.

Mr. Williams: Oh, yes, and I am coming to place an order with you. We like the design of your bamboo chopsticks.

Mr. Bai: We will send you ___2___ soon. But there are few questions sought to be settled first. Say, the cost for sending the goods.

Mr. Williams: I am listening.

Mr. Bai: You see, we quoted you as warehouse price. If you want me to give you the price FOB, that would _____3_____, leaving you to pay the sea freights and marine insurance. Is that what you want?

Mr. Williams: No. I think we should prefer to have an idea of the total costs delivering right to our port.

Mr. Bai: Then what about a CIF price? That would cover the cost of the goods from warehouse to warehouse.

Mr. Williams: But there will be a few things left for us to pay.

Mr. Bai: Yes, the charges …for your forward agent for _____4_____. I can get the CIF prices worked out when we go on talking. Miss Yang, take this price quotation to the shipping department and get them to work out CIF prices for Mr. Williams, will you?

Mr. Williams: I appreciate your working efficiency, Mr. Bai. I am afraid there is another issue to be discussed, the delivery. How soon can it be effected?

Mr. Bai: We will take partial deliveries. I mean, _____5_____. And this can be dispatched just as soon as we can get the shipping space. In this case, I suggest you make your order in two, with the interval of 3 weeks.

Mr. Williams: Good.

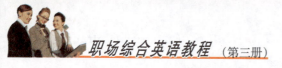

Mr. Bai:	And the second consignment would be forwarded when the goods are available from the factory.
Mr. Williams:	Excuse me, but we should like to have the definite date for the last shipment.
Mr. Bai:	Of course. In the LC the shipping date will be made clear, saying no later than a certain date, which is determined by our supply.
Mr. Williams:	Good. That is I know the best way.
Mr. Bai:	That depends on our production program. But you are not pressed for time, aren't you?
Mr. Williams:	Oh, no.
Mr. Bai:	Good, well. While Miss Yang is typing out this quotation, perhaps you'll have something to drink with me.
Mr. Williams:	Thank you very much. I should like to.

Exercise 4

Directions: You will hear a short passage. Listen carefully and decide whether the following statements are true or false.

_____ 1. Negotiation is commonly used in business.

_____ 2. You don't have to negotiate with the governments.

_____ 3. The fact that different interests exist means you have to negotiate with everybody.

_____ 4. Many businesses are regulated by contract.

_____ 5. When preparing a new contract, negotiation sometimes can be omitted.

Task 2   Oral Practice

Warming-up Questions:

1. What do you think are the effective ways to collect business information?
2. What is trade fair? Do you have any idea about the Canton Fair?
3. What kind of role do you think China is playing in the field of international business?

Exercise 1

Directions: Read the brochure of a piping making company and try to answer the following questions.

* ultraslide 超滑   leakage-free 无渗漏   fitting tooth 配件齿
  sleeve 套管   spring 弹簧

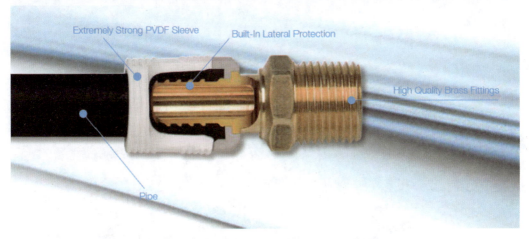

Sagiv UltraSlide™

Innovative slide pipe fitting system for all PEX & PE-RT pipe types, that is reliable, easy to use, and allows for leakage-free installation.
The UltraSlide eliminates the need for O-Ring, and uses a patented sealing technology based on the penetration of the fitting tooth into the pipe surface, and an extremely strong sleeve that functions as a spring, keeping the connection area tidy and 'Dry-Forever'.

1. What is the name of the company?

2. What is the main product of the company?

3. What are the essential features of the products?

Exercise 2

Directions: Read another piece of the brochure and try to make a presentation for the latest product about its structure, features or installation.

Technology • O-Ring Free • Easy-to-use • Single Tool • Leakage Free

THE UltraSlide™ PIPE FITTING SYSTEM INCLUDES:
High quality Brass fittings & PVDF Sleeves

Innovative single-step operation tools

THE UltraSlide™ SYSTEM IN OPERATION:

Cut the pipe | Set the fitting and the pipe in the tool | Connect the fitting and the sleeve to the pipe - in single step | Done

Part II Reading

Text A

Before Reading:
Work in groups and say something about Red Bull.

Red Bull Gives You a Business Strategy

In the summer of 1982, thirty-six-year-old Austrian toothpaste salesman Dietrich Mateschitz boarded a plane for a routine business trip to Thailand. There was nothing about Mateschitz at the moment that would have tipped you off that he was about to make a discovery that would make him one of the world's wealthiest men and create a new kind of company that conveys its story in a new way — through actions and experiences.

As luck would have it, Mateschitz arrived jet-lagged. Some locals took pity on him and directed him to a store where he was told to ask for an exotic-sounding tonic called Krating Daeng. Mateschitz learned that Krating Daeng was prized by locals for its ability to increase physical endurance and mental concentration.

Are you still having trouble guessing the identity of this company? It might help to know that the Thai name Krating Daeng translates roughly in English to "red bull". Upon making his discovery, Mateschitz sought out the manufacturer of Krating Daeng and with passion and persistence convinced him that there was a vast market outside Thailand for Red Bull. The two formed Red Bull GmbH and set to work on a product formulation and a marketing plan to pursue a specific group of people: young men aged eighteen to thirty-four who were enthusiasts of a growing movement — adventure sports. In 1987, the first can of Red Bull energy drink went on sale in Mateschitz's native Austria.

This is where it starts to get interesting because here Mateschitz reveals his one true superpower. It turns out that hiding inside the mild-mannered toothpaste salesman was an extraordinarily talented storyteller and experiential marketer. Mateschitz didn't have a large amount of TV budget. He had something much more important — a vision. He believed Red Bull could become something far greater than liquid in a can. From the very beginning, Mateschitz viewed Red Bull as a lifestyle, a kind of belief system, a religion in which that can of liquid was necessary and functional.

Like many entrepreneurs before him, Mateschitz had the vision clearly in his head, but he didn't find the right execution on Day one. The breakout moment for Red Bull came in 1990, when Mateschitz came up with an event he called the Red Bull Flugtag ("flight day" or "air show" in German).

Thirty years later, Red Bull has become a company that is hard to describe in conventional terms and perhaps the premier global example of a business that combines story and action — something I call a storydoing company. Instead of "telling" its story using advertising, Red Bull conveys its story through the creation of compelling experiences, all carefully crafted to "give you wings". Because of this, Red Bull has become a packaged-goods company that is also a content creation company that is also an events company that is also an adventure sports lifestyle company.

Stories live in the hearts of human beings and in the future, and should be at the core of every business. The truth is you have the power to become an agent of change in your own organization today. You just have to roll up your sleeves and get to work.

New Words

jet-lagged	/dʒet'lagd/	adj.	有时差反应的
exotic	/ɪɡ'zɒtɪk/	adj.	异国的;外来的
endurance	/ɪn'djʊərəns/	n.	持久(力);忍耐,忍耐力
concentration	/ˌkɒnsn'treɪʃn/	n.	集中;专心;关注;浓度
formulation	/ˌfɔːmjʊ'leɪʃn/	n.	配方;构想
enthusiast	/ɪn'θjuːzɪast/	n.	热衷于……的人;狂热者
extraordinarily	/ɪk'strɔːdnrəlɪ/	adv.	特别,极其;离奇地
vision	/'vɪʒn/	n.	视力,视觉;美景;想像力
execution	/ˌɛksɪ'kjuːʃ(ə)n/	n.	实行,履行,执行,贯彻
premier	/'prɛmɪə/	adj.	第一的,首位的
compelling	/kəm'pɛlɪŋ/	adj.	引人入胜的;非常强烈的;不可抗拒的

Phrases and Expressions

tip off	暗示,警告
take pity on	同情
seek out	找出,物色
come up with	追赶上;比得上;想出

Unit 6 Business Contact

Proper Names

* GmbH　　　（Gesellschaft mit beschraenkter Haftung）是德国、奥地利、瑞士等国家的一种公司组织形式，类似于美国的有限责任公司（Limitted Liability Company, LLC）

Exercises

I. Answer the following questions according to the passage.

1. Why was Mateschitz introduced to try a special drinking?

2. Why is Krating Daeng well-known among the local people?

3. What are the target customers of the Red Bull?

4. What was the breakthrough of the Red Bull?

5. What is the secret of the success of the Red Bull?

II. Fill in the blanks with the proper words and expressions given below, changing the form if necessary.

routine	convey	exotic	endurance	convince
extraordinarily	experiential	execution	compelling	premier

1. His music _____ a sense of optimism.
2. The idea was never put into _____.
3. The company has achieved a _____ position in the electronics field.
4. Long-distance races are won by the runners with the greatest _____.
5. They failed to _____ the directors that their proposals would work.
6. Maybe we should change the work, as you are more _____ than me.
7. It's a _____ medical examination, nothing to get worried about.
8. He is telling his _____ adventure story.
9. The girl wearing an _____ dress comes from India.
10. It took an _____ long time.

83

III. Translate the following sentences into Chinese.

1. There was nothing about Mateschitz at the moment that would have tipped you off that he was about to make a discovery that would make him one of the world's wealthiest men and create a new kind of company.
2. Some locals took pity on him and directed him to a store where he was told to ask for an exotic-sounding tonic.
3. It turns out that hiding inside the mild-mannered toothpaste salesman was an extraordinarily talented storyteller and experiential marketer.
4. Instead of "telling" its story using advertising, Red Bull conveys its story through the creation of compelling experiences.

IV. Translate the following sentences into English.

1. 结果比我们原先设想的还要好。
2. 就像很多农民所做的那样，我的祖父也常常同情那些饥饿的野鸡，把玉米和小米撒在外面，让它们和其他鸟类来吃。
3. 我们容纳不同的文化，我们寻求创新的意念和处事方式。
4. 董事会费尽心思讨论了一下午，最终找到了一个解决问题的好办法。

Text B

Before Reading:

1. Have you ever complained about some company or service?
2. If you are a manager of a supermarket, how would you deal with a customer's complaint?

Ten Ways to Handle Customer's Complaint

Most clients don't complain. Often if they are dissatisfied they just stop doing business with you. If a client does complain about you or your service however they are doing you a service and enabling you to improve your business. Here are some tips on handling the complaint:

1. Listen.

Resist the *temptation* to argue with the client. Instead ask questions to *get to the bottom* of the situation. What is the client really upset about? *Rephrase* what the client says so he/she knows you understand the issue.

2. Don't be defensive.

This will get in the way of your listening to the client. Allow the client the time to be heard. If you get *defensive* you'll build a wall between you and the client. Try to find ways to build a bridge so that you are *aligned with* the client.

3. If it was your mistake fix it immediately and apologize.

We all make mistakes at times. Check to see if there is anything in your office procedure that can help you to avoid a similar mistake again.

4. Research the problem before you make any decisions.

Find out what actually happened. Is a system in your office not working correctly? Does it need to be fixed? Has the client misunderstood something? For complex problems give yourself time to figure out a resolution.

5. Look for lessons in the situation.

If the situation was caused by something you or your staff control, find a way to fix it for the future. This means assessing the systems you have in place and your methods and procedures. It also may mean retraining an employee or employees.

6. Reeducate the client when necessary.

How did you set client expectations? Were you clear about what he / she could expect? Help the client to understand the process now to guard against future misunderstandings.

7. Know that if one client complained there are others feeling the same way.

What do you need to do to address the problem with the others? Who else might have been affected in the same way?

8. Give client choice of possible resolutions.

How can you make this right with the client? Negotiate a way that works for both of you. Sometimes just fixing the problem is sufficient. At other times the client is looking for something else. Look for an equitable resolution.

9. Thank the client for helping you with your business.

As painful as they can be, complaints from clients often let you know exactly where you need to work to improve your practice.

10. Follow up with those who complained to be sure they are fully satisfied.

If you have altered a system or changed a way of doing business and the client is affected by that change, follow up to be sure that the client noted the change.

New Words

complaint	/kəmˈpleɪnt/	n.	抱怨;疾病;诉苦;控告;投诉
temptation	/tem(p)ˈteɪʃ(ə)n/	n.	诱惑;引诱物
rephrase	/ˌriːˈfreɪz/	vt.	重新措辞;改述
defensive	/dɪˈfensɪv/	adj.	防卫的;防御的;辩护的
		n.	防卫姿势;防卫物
resolution	/rezəˈluːʃ(ə)n/	n.	决心;决定;解决;决议;坚决;分辨率
assess	/əˈses/	v.	评定;评估;估算
sufficient	/səˈfɪʃ(ə)nt/	adj.	足够的;充分的
equitable	/ˈekwɪtəb(ə)l/	adj.	公平的;公正的

Phrases and Expressions

get to the bottom	追根究底；到达尽头；彻底查明
align with	结盟；使密切合作；使一致；匹配
figure out	算出；想出；解决；理解；断定
guard against	防止；防范
follow up	跟进；采取措施

Exercises

I. Read the above passage carefully and decide whether the following statements are true or false.

_____ 1. Stopping doing business can also be seen as a complaint.
_____ 2. We should argue with the customers to make it clear what is going on.
_____ 3. Check to see if there is anything in your office procedure that can help you to avoid a similar mistake again.
_____ 4. One complaint from a customer does not mean that others will have the same feeling.
_____ 5. Complaints from clients often let you know exactly where you need to work to improve your practice.

II. Fill in the blanks with the proper words and expressions given below, changing the form if necessary.

satisfy	resolution	upset	sufficient	alter
defend	temptation	assess	note	affect

1. Troops took up a _____ position around the town.
2. We have passed a _____ to build a new laboratory.
3. We should equitably _____ historical figures.
4. The police have _____ evidence to connect the suspect with the explosion.
5. More than seven million people have been _____ by drought.
6. I shall never feel _____ until that debt is wiped off.
7. Push against _____ and you will get muscle in your character.
8. She was very _____ at what to him was just a throwaway remark.
9. Suddenly, I _____ that the rain had stopped.
10. They have never _____ their programs by a single day.

III. Pay attention to different parts of speech and select the appropriate word to fill in the blank.

1. complain, complaint, complainer, complainingly
   a. She never _____, but she's obviously exhausted.
   b. He was a terrible _____ — always moaning about something.
   c. She did her work, but she did so _____.
   d. We received a number of _____ from customers about the lack of parking facilities.
2. apology, apologize
   a. You should make an _____ to her for your carelessness.
   b. We _____ for any inconvenience it may have caused.
3. expect, expectation, expectable, unexpected
   a. The result shows that Chinese money maze rate would gradually decrease in the _____ future.
   b. Things were working well when we were brought up against _____ delays.
   c. I didn't _____ to be given the red carpet treatment!
   d. The beauties of the West Lake in spring were beyond his _____.
4. affect (v.), affect (n.), affection
   a. The dog has transferred its _____ to its new master.
   b. You never allow personal problems to _____ your performance.
   c. Until the 1960s, people began to pay attention to the function of _____ in language teaching.

IV. Class Work

The client is not satisfied with the products and making the complaints, while the seller is trying to solve the business dispute. Work in pairs and make a role play.

Part III Writing

Memo

A memo is intended to inform a group of people about a specific issue, such as an event, policy, or resource, and encourages them to take action. The word "memorandum" means something that should be remembered or kept in mind.

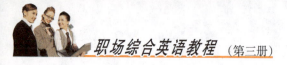

Sample 1

MEMORANDUM

From: Olive HR Manager
To: All staff
Date: 12 June, 2013
Subject: Appointment of Francisco

　　Here we announce the appointment of Mrs. Francisco as our new Sales Manager of the Headquarter. She will be starting her job next Monday morning. There will be a small welcome party by 9:00 that day, so everyone please be on time.

Sample 2

To: Customers of Chloe's Cupcakes
From: Dan Lionel, Public Relations Liaison
Date: May 12, 2012
Subject: Publication of Nutrition Facts

　　Due to extensive customer feedback, we at Chloe's Cupcakes would like to demonstrate our commitment to making healthy choices by publishing nutrition information for all of our baked goods.

　　We are confident that you, the customer, will feel better about choosing Chloe's Cupcakes once you are aware of these facts. We are committed to use the best locally grown ingredients in our baked goods, and we freshly prepare all of our desserts each morning. Moreover, we have a line of vegan treats that substitute some of the highest-calorie ingredients in non-vegan goods with healthier options—while still delivering great flavor.

　　All of our nutrition information will be available online, along with a list of ingredients and possible substitutes for those with dietary restrictions. We will also provide pamphlets in stores with the same information, to be updated periodically. However, we are unable to guarantee access to nutritional information for seasonal flavors and promotional items.

Best,
Dan Lionel

Unit 6 Business Contact

Exercise:

> **Situation:** You are the Managing Director of a company whose profits have recently increased and you would like to reward staff for this.
>
> Write a memo to all staff: thanking them for their contribution; explaining why profits increased; telling them what their reward will be.

Part IV Cultural Express

Direction: Read the text about the business partnership. What is the significance of partnership? Could you give some actual examples?

How to Form a Business Partnership

A business partnership is an agreement between two or more individuals to operate a business jointly. Partners are responsible for the other partner's business actions, as well as their own.

1. To form a business partnership.
2. List the amount of equity to be invested by each partner.
3. Determine how the profit or loss will be divided among the partners.
4. Establish compensation levels for each partner, including when the compensation will be given and any restrictions that might affect that compensation.
5. Set guidelines for how the business will be modified or dissolved should one or more partners wish to end the partnership.
6. Define procedures for settling any disputes which might arise.
7. Determine who has authority for which expenditures and how expenditure decisions are to be made.
8. Develop procedures to follow in case of death or incapacitation of a partner.
9. Write and sign an agreement detailing the responses to the questions above.

A general partnership can be formed simply by an oral agreement, but a legal partnership agreement drawn up by an attorney is highly recommended.

Tips:

1. Equity can be cash, physical assets or skills. Skills are an intangible asset to which a value should be assigned.
2. In a Limited Partnership limited partners have limited personal liability for business debts as long as they do not participate in management.
3. The partners report their share of profit or loss on their personal tax returns.

Supplementary Vocabulary

dumping	商品倾销
free trade zone	自由贸易区
customs duty	关税
price including commission	含佣价
spot price	现货价格
forward price	期货价格
shipper, consignor	托运人
consignee	收货人
clearance of goods	报关
to take delivery of goods	提货
price indication	指示性价格
usual practice	习惯做法
time of validity	有效期限
submission of tender	投标
exclusive right	独家经营/专营权
fair average quality	大路货(良好平均品质)
arbitration	仲裁
inspection certificate	品质、重量检验证书
foreign exchange	外汇
rate of exchange	汇率
net weight	净重
gross weight	毛重

Unit 7

Automobile

Learning Objectives:

You are able to:

☞ Know Auto's culture and history

☞ Learn to be a successful car salesman

☞ Learn how to effectively communicate with your potential customers

☞ Get to know the writing skills of table/graph composition and the whole procedure of car purchase

Language Focus

anti-lock brake	防抱死制动
cruise control	恒速操纵器
malfunction	故障,失灵
pedal	踩踏板
lever	控制杆
steering wheel	方向盘
rear-view mirror	后视镜
switch on	接通,开启
ignition	点火开关/装置

Part I Listening and Speaking

Task 1 Listening Practice

Exercise 1   A dialogue between Nick and a car salesman named John in a 4S store

Directions: Now you will hear a short dialogue. Listen carefully and choose the best answer from the four choices.

1. The customer would like to choose _____ the salesman showed him before..
   A. Honda Spirior   B. Honda Fit   C. Honda Accord   D. Honda Civic
2. The standards of the new car include the following items, except _____.
   A. air conditioning   B. brake assist   C. anti-lock brakes D. a CD player
3. The Accord comes with cruise control, however, the customer thinks it is _____.
   A. impractical   B. difficult   C. unreliable   D. dangerous
4. If the man order one now, he would get the new car _____.
   A. in September   B. in August   C. in April   D. in March

Exercise 2   A conversation between a driving instructor and a learner

Directions: Now you will hear a conversation. You are required to put in the missing information.

Instructor:	Ok, so you are sitting in the car. What do you do now?
Learner:	Well, I start the car. No, wait! I check behind me first before I drive away.
Instructor:	You've forgotten something.
Learner:	Of course, I fasten my ___1___ first.
Instructor:	Even before you fasten your seat belt there are things you need to do. First of all, are you sitting comfortably?
Learner:	Not really. The seat is a bit ___2___ the pedals.
Instructor:	So you need to adjust the seat, right? Use ___3___ there to adjust the position and the height. You can also adjust the steering wheel. So now you're sitting comfortably. What should you check now?
Learner:	That ___4___ is in the right position. And the side mirror.
Instructor:	Quite right. What next?
Learner:	Well, if it's dark, I need to switch on the headlights.
Instructor:	Good. Finally, before you ___5___ the ignition, what should you do?
Learner:	Now I fasten my seat belt.

Exercise 3

Directions: Now you will hear a passage. You are required to put in the missing information.

While automobiles are a ____1____ part of any transportation system, car culture makes it difficult to create sustainable urban transport. When consumer demand calls for size and horsepower — not ____2____ or ____3____ — fuel efficiency is quickly sacrificed. Moreover, when cars become so ____4____ valued rather than simply functionally important, necessary ____5____ for sustainable transport become difficult.

Exercise 4

Directions: Now you will hear a short passage. Listen carefully and decide whether the following statements are true or false.

_____ 1. One out of seven Americans works at making cars, driving trucks, building roads or filling up gas.
_____ 2. Most Americans can live without cars.
_____ 3. The polluted air is poisonous and dangerous to health
_____ 4. It is easy to build a clean car practically.
_____ 5. Inventors are now working on steam cars and electric cars.

Task 2 Oral Practice

Exercise 1

Directions: Suppose you're a car salesman. You're going to introduce a new car to your customer. Follow the sample to make a conversation with your partner.

Salesman: Good morning, sir! Can I help you?
Customer: Yes. Um ... I'd like to buy a SUV. What's your recommendation?
Salesman: Sure. This way, please.
Salesman: This is Freelander, sir !
Customer: Wow! It is cool! It has a Straightforward atmosphere look.
Salesman: Yes. Would you like to look at the interior?
Customer: Sure.
Salesman: The new interior still continues the Freelander design style of the preceding paragraph, the line is flat, hale, function keys amount is more and more decentralized distribution, which is beneficial to the winter wear gloves to the owner of the vehicle.
Customer: Yes. It is great. Well, how about the engine performance and engine displacement?
Salesman: The engines maximum power is 177kW at 5,500rpm. And the engine displacement is 3192 ml.
Customer: Um ... May I have a test drive ?

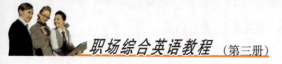

Salesman: Sure. Could you show me your driving license?
Customer: Yes. Here it is.

Exercise 2

Directions: Now you see a car company advertisement. Suppose you are the Manager of the company. A customer comes to ask you for information about your company. Be prepared to answer his or her questions.

Sol Cars

Small, two-door car
Medium sized, two-door car
Medium sized, four-door car
Luxury, four-door car
Luxury sports car

Buy: With one-year guarantee and servicing
       With a three-year guarantee and servicing

Rent: One-, two- or three-year rental periods
       includes servicing
       Can also include insurance

Part II Reading

Text A

Before Reading:
1. Do you know any German car brands? Can you give some examples?
2. Who invented the first gasoline car in the world?

Audi's New Dynamism

Even before the new company group was established, Audi's design office had drawn up plans for a new model. It was to have front-wheel drive and a six-cylinder engine. The most suitable source of power was considered to be the new 40 bhp Wanderer engine designed by Ferdinand Porsche. Its low weight of 130 kilograms was another point in its favor.

To keep the complete car as light as possible, a box-section chassis frame was used, which in turn encouraged the designers to adopt independent suspension at the front and rear.

Auto Union exhibited this new Audi Front model at the 1933 International Car and Motorcycle Show in Berlin. Together with Stoewer and Brennabor, the brand thus paved the way for front-wheel drive to become accepted in the medium-size car class.

Audi customers at that time were primarily interested in comfort, convenience and ample space rather than sheer performance. By the mid-1930s a change had set in: dynamism and sporting character gained in importance—the car should be powerful, but not too large. In accordance with company policy, the new Audi was again to feature extremely progressive design elements. Jaray's streamlined body outlines were considered, together with pulsating-action automatic transmission. The car was to be aimed at a specific buyer group with greater awareness of automobile engineering development — one that would appreciate the technical merits of a car designed for sporty day-to-day driving, and one that possessed the necessary financial resources to adopt this approach.

In view of all this, the designers had to find more power from somewhere. The Wanderer engines had now been uprated to 55 bhp and could not be developed any further. The front-wheel-drive shaft joints, too, were rated for a maximum operating life of 30,000 kilometers. Since a top speed of well over 120 km/h was targeted, the only option was to revert to conventional rear-wheel drive. The new Audi 920 was the work of Auto Union's Central Development and Design Department in Chemnitz; since early 1934, Audi had had no design office of its own. Instead of being able to adopt unusual technical features, and also because of the industry's permanent shortage of raw materials and the resulting delays in development schedules, there was no alternative but to be content with a modified standard body and various other well-proven design elements, the new six-cylinder OHC engine had a power output of 75 bhp, enough to give the car a top speed of more than 130 km/h.

New Words

dynamism	/ˈdʌɪnəmɪz(ə)m/	n.	活力;动态;推动力
bhp		abbr.	制动马力(Brake Horse Power)
ample	/ˈamp(ə)l/	adj.	丰富的;足够的;宽敞的
sheer	/ʃɪə/	adj.	绝对的;透明的;峻峭的;纯粹的
progressive	/prəˈgrɛsɪv/	adj.	进步的;先进的

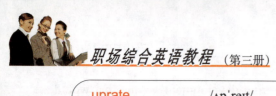

uprate	/ʌpˈreɪt/	v.	提高……的等级；改进性能；提高价值
revert	/rɪˈvɜːt/	v.	回复；重提；归还（常与 to 连用）
conventional	/kənˈvenʃ(ə)n(ə)l/	adj.	符合习俗的，传统的；常见的；惯例的
modified	/ˈmɒdɪfʌɪd/	adj.	改进的，修改的；改良的
permanent	/ˈpɜːm(ə)nənt/	adj.	永久的，永恒的；不变的
alternative	/ɔːlˈtəːnətɪv/	adj.	供选择的；选择性的；交替的
		n.	二中择一；供替代的选择
OHC		abbr.	凸轮轴（Overhead camshaft）

Phrases and Expressions

draw up	草拟，起草；停住；使靠近
in one's favor	对……有利；受到……欢迎
in accordance with	依照；与……一致
front-wheel drive	前轮驱动
six-cylinder	六个气缸的
box-section	箱形截面
chassis frame	汽车车架；底盘架构
independent suspension	[机]独立悬架，独立悬挂
front and rear	在前后
streamlined body	流线型体
pulsating-action	脉动作用
automatic transmission	自动换档；自动变速装置
technical merits	技术水平；技术得分；技术点
In view of	鉴于；考虑到
shaft joint	联轴器
rear-wheel drive	后轮驱动
be content with	以……为满足；满足于

• Unit 7 Automobile •

Proper Names	
Wanderer	流浪者；漫游者；奥迪四环徽标之一的德国漫游者汽车公司
Stoewer	斯维托尔……德国著名汽车品牌
Brennabor	德国兰牌自行车
Jaray	瑞士空气动力学家保罗·杰瑞 (Paul Jaray)
Chemnitz	开姆尼斯（德国萨克森州西部的一个城市）

Exercises

I. Answer the following questions according to the passage.

1. What are the features of the new model by Audi's design office before the new company group was established?
   _____

2. Where did Audi Union exhibit the New Front Model?
   _____

3. At that time, what would better arouse Audi customers' interests for new cars?
   _____

4. By the mid-1930s, which buyer group should be aimed at with the new change?
   _____

5. From the last paragraph of this passage, what is the new breakthrough for the car power research?
   _____

II. Fill in the blanks with the proper words and expressions given below, changing the form if necessary.

dynamism	revert	modified	in accordance with
be content with	front and rear	in view of	progressive
permanent	uprate		

1. We must not _____ such a small success.
2. She has been granted _____ residency in Britain.
3. After having talked about some household affairs for a long while, we _____ to the original topic.
4. _____ the above — mentioned facts, we wish to make the following proposals.

5. _____ this plan, we shall look for the first payment on Sept.1.
6. It is this energetic feedback and element of anticipation that gives jazz its incredible _____.
7. Whichever one you fancy, _____ bumpers both match the body color.
8. The industrial revolution _____ the whole structure of English society.
9. There has been a _____ decrease in population every year in this city.
10. Our old-age pension will be _____ next month.

III. Translate the following sentences into Chinese.

1. The most suitable source of power was considered to be the new 40 bhp Wanderer engine designed by Ferdinand Porsche.
2. To keep the complete car as light as possible, a box-section chassis frame was used, which in turn encouraged the designers to adopt independent suspension at the front and rear.
3. In accordance with company policy, the new Audi was again to feature extremely progressive design elements.
4. Since a top speed of well over 120 km/h was targeted, the only option was to revert to conventional rear-wheel drive.

IV. Translate the following sentences into English.

1. 你们应按照规则进行比赛。(*in accordance with*)
2. 上了年纪的人视力逐步减退。(*progressive*)
3. 他们开了几次会来制定今年的生产计划。(*draw up*)
4. 发动机经过改良升级可以产生更大的动力。(*uprate*)

Text B

Before Reading:
1. What are the job duties of being a car salesman/saleswoman?
2. Would you like to take a job as a car salesman/saleswoman in the future?

You Should Think About a Job Selling Cars

Think about a job a car salesman, you should? Having a career in car sales can be a good career. Being a car salesman is not the career choice of many people although it can be fulfilling. There are many people selling cars that make good money. I have known many that make over 100K a year selling cars.

The career of a car salesman is not for just anybody, drive and ambition is required to succeed. You could go to college, get a degree and still not earn the income of a good car salesman. You can't beat a college education, but just like selling cars it's not for everybody. If college is not an option *available* to you, consider selling cars for a living.

Like any new job, it takes a short amount of time to adjust. You will require to get comfortable with the car business in order to become a great car sales person. Whatever your ambition might be, it takes a few months to adjust before you start earning the real money. When you start selling cars for a car dealership, they typically provide some basic car sales training to get you started in the right direction.

A car sales career usually demands you to work 50 or more hours a week at least, the potential for 100K a year helps make up for the hours. Working more than 40 hours a week is very common for most jobs with a good income. The average day for a car salesman is not hard work, not in the physical sense. You won't get sweaty and dirty from selling cars, in fact you can be well dressed everyday.

The daily life of a car salesman includes taking customers on test drives, negotiating and building rapport. There might be cases where you would pickup a trade-in, fill out credit applications or make a trade with another dealer. Just like any job you will have good days and bad days, but there are usually more good than bad. There are ups and downs like any job, but selling cars for a living is one of the easier jobs you will have.

There is a downside to having a career in car sales. The paycheck of a car salesman can vary based on commission. The auto sales pro is paid all commission which can cause variations in the pay, but overall a top salesman can make good money. Holidays can be a big day for selling cars and many sales people consider that a negative. When it comes down to earning 100K a year without a college degree, car sales might be a good choice. So, when you are pounding the pavement looking for a job, selling cars for a living is something you should consider.

New Words

available	/əˈveɪləb(ə)l/	adj.	有效的,可得的;可利用的;空闲的
dealership	/ˈdiːləʃɪp/	n.	代理权;代理商;经销权
sweaty	/ˈswɛti/	adj.	出汗的;吃力的;使人出汗的
rapport	/raˈpɔː/	n.	密切关系,交往;和谐一致
trade-in	/ˈtreɪdɪn/	n.	折价物;折合价
downside	/ˈdaʊnsʌɪd/	n.	下降趋势;底侧;缺点
paycheck	/ˈpeɪˌtʃɛk/	n.	付薪水的支票,薪水
commission	/kəˈmɪʃ(ə)n/	n.	佣金

Phrases and Expressions

physical sense	物理/身体感受
test drive	试验驾驶，试车
credit application	信贷申请表
ups and downs	沉浮；盛衰；高低
come down to	归根结底，可归结为；实质上是
pound the pavement	徘徊街头

Exercises

I. Read the above passage carefully and decide whether the following statements are true or false.

____ 1. Nothing is required to anyone who wants to be a car salesman.

____ 2. If you go to college and get a degree, it is possible for you not to earn quite enough compared to a car salesman.

____ 3. The average day for a car salesman is really hard work, especially in their physical sense.

____ 4. Any job has ups and downs, however, selling cars for a living is a relatively easier one.

____ 5. Most sales people would consider that holidays could be a big day for car sales.

II. Fill in the blanks with the proper words and expressions given below, changing the form if necessary.

| available | sweaty | pro | ups and downs | come down to |
| rapport | commission | dealership | paycheck | trade-in |

1. Every one must have his share of the _____.
2. Brian set his heart on becoming a _____ baseball player.
3. The car _____ did brisk business this weekend, selling over 50 vehicles.
4. My bicycle is not _____, and it is being repaired.
5. He question _____ whether we ought to act upon his advice.
6. Are you not satisfied with your current _____?
7. Carrying such a heavy bag, I was very easy to get _____.
8. He bought a _____ for a low price.
9. She has an excellent _____ with her staff.
10. The salesman can get _____ on everything he sells.

III. Pay attention to different parts of speech and select the appropriate word to fill in the blank.

1. ambition, ambitious, ambitiousness
   a. She's _____ and eager to be successful.
   b. The realization of his _____ makes him very happy.
   c. He not only has dedication, _____ and youth, but also has the courage.
2. avail, available, availability
   a. The _____ of cheap long - term credit would help small business.
   b. All his efforts did not _____.
   c. If possible, you should examine all data fields _____.
3. apply, applicable, application
   a. This rule is not _____ to foreigners.
   b. Fill in your address at the bottom of the _____ form.
   c. I made up my mind to _____ for a scholarship.
4. direct(v.), direct(adj.), director, direction,
   a. Which is the most _____ way to London?
   b. He realized that he was heading in the wrong _____.
   c. The general _____ that the prisoners should be set free.
   d. The _____ told the actress to have a rest.
5. vary, variety, various, variation
   a. Prices have not shown much _____ this year.
   b. He decided to leave school for _____ reasons.
   c. Rents _____ from a few hundred dollars to thousands in large cities.
   d. There're a large _____ of goods in the shops.

IV. Class Work

According to the description of the career as a car salesman, would you like to take this job after your graduation? Give your own reasons.

Part III Writing

Task 1

Table/Graph Composition

This kind of writing is an information interpretation process. The information may be given in numbers, lines or curves, etc., usually a few explanations are given. The organization of the writing is essential to a good essay of tables and graphs. Generally, it is as follows: General introduction — Analysis — Conclusion

Sample 1:

Accidents in a Chinese city

Main accident causes	Number of accidents 2005	Percentage rise(+) or fall(−)
Drivers turning left without due care	608	+10%
Drivers turning too close to other vehicles	411	+9%
Pedestrians crossing roads carelessly	401	+12%
Drivers driving under the influence of alcohol	281	+15%
Drivers failing to give a signal	264	−5%

Directions: You are required to write an essay based on the following table. Describe the table and state your opinion. You should write at least 150 words.

Reference：(Pay attention to the underlined words, phrases and sentences)

As is shown in the table, the traffic accidents in 2005 add up to 1965 and increase by approximately 10 percent. Apparently, the number of traffic accidents dramatically increased in 2005 compared with the previous year.

What accounts for the increase? In the light of the table, we can find that a couple of factors contribute to the change. To begin with, drivers' careless driving behaviors are mainly responsible for the traffic accidents. Among them turning left without care gives rise to the most accidents of 608, while driving under the influence of alcohol leads to the highest accident increase rate. In addition, the increase of the accidents has something to do with pedestrians' careless behavior. Pedestrians' crossing roads carelessly is blamed for 401 accidents and causes an increase rate of 12 percent. Drivers' ill driving habits such as failing to give a signal also result in traffic accidents, though the accident rate slightly decreases.

Now that we are aware of the causes of the traffic accidents and the increase of them, it is time for us to work out measures to cut down the number. With strict driving regulations and education to drivers and pedestrians, the traffic accidents are expected to fall off and we are expected to live in a secure traffic environment.

Unit 7 Automobile

Exercise:

Directions: Write an essay based on the following chart. In your writing, you should interpret the chart and give your comments. You should write at least 150 words.

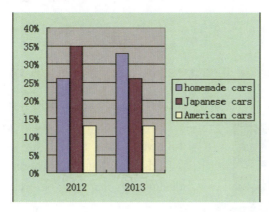

Task 2

Here is a sample of Vehicle Sales Flowchart. Translate the following steps into corresponding Chinese expressions and try your best to learn the eight steps by your heart.

1. _____
2. _____
3. _____
4. _____
5. _____
6. _____
7. _____
8. _____

Part IV Cultural Express

Directions: Read the text about the latest fashion of Beetle. What new features have been mentioned about the latest one?

Beetle — 2014 VW Beetle Features — Volkswagen of America

Retro cool meets modern style

19-inch alloy wheels

Take a look at the bolder Beetle. It's sportier and more aggressive, thanks in part to the available 19" performance alloy wheels that stare right back at you. They're wrapped in high-performance rubber that won't just give your Beetle a whole new look, they'll give you goose bumps when you hit the road.

17-inch Turbine wheels

If these wheels look fast now, imagine what they'll look like flying down the highway. Take a peek at the 17" Turbine wheels on the Volkswagen Beetle. Their design says fast even before you step on the gas.

Classic design

Take a nice long look. The sleek, arcing profile is known the world over. The front end, with its familiar headlights, is instantly recognizable. We made the 2014 Beetle simple because that's how it's always been. And always will be. Sure, we gave it a sportier stance by shaving a bit off the top and stretched the hood slightly. But you can see both the original and new designs in every angle, whether you spot it directly ahead or from the behind the wheel. Because even though it sports a sleek update, a classic never goes out of style.

Bi-Xenon headlights

Brighter than halogen or regular filament bulbs, light from the available

Bi-Xenon headlights is created by an arc of electricity inside the bulb that's filled with xenon gas. These lights also boast a longer life. The Adaptive Front-lighting System (AFS) comes standard with the Bi-Xenon headlights and can turn the headlights up to 15 degrees to help you see things in a whole new light.

Keyless access with push-button start

With available keyless access, keep your keys in your pocket — the door on your Beetle will automatically unlock as you grip the door handle. Then, once you're inside, a simple press of the brake and the start button turns on the ignition so you're ready to go. Ready to lock up? Just press the lock sensor on the outside door handle. The most convenient key of all is one you don't have to touch.

Supplementary Vocabulary

acceleration	加速,加速度
aerial	天线
aerodynamic	流行型,空气动力学的
air conditioning	空气调节系统,空调
assembly line	装配线,流水作业线
audio system	音频系统,放声装置
automatic parking system	汽车自动停车系统
blind	百叶窗
body panel	汽车配件
body shell	车身外壳
body-in-white	未油漆的车身
boot	(汽车后部的)行李箱
brake assist	制动增力装置
bumper	(汽车车身前后的)保险杠
camera monitoring	摄像监控
camper van	露营用房车
car sharing	拼车,汽车共享服务

car wash	洗车处
clutch pedal	离合器踏板
containment action	补救措施
controller	控制装置
convertible	折篷轿车
cost-effective	划算的，价格上有利的
coupe	双门小轿车
engine oil	机油，发动机润滑油
estate	旅行汽车
exhaust gases	废气
fender	保险杠，挡泥板
fog light	雾天前照灯
head-on collision	正面相撞

Unit 8

E-commerce

Learning Objectives:

You are able to:

☞ Be familiar with the basic concepts of E-commerce

☞ Be aware of the advantages and disadvantages of E-money

☞ Know the process of Internet marketing

☞ Write order letters

☞ Know some information about famous E-commerce sites

Language Focus

dispatch	配货	delivery	送货
return	退货	refund	退款
exchange	换货		
check the status of your refund/ return	查看退款/退货状态		
order	订货/下订单	change your order	修改订单
track your parcel	跟踪包裹	payment	付款
print an invoice	打印发票	cancel items or orders	取消购物/订单
manage payment methods	管理付款方式		
manage your address	管理收货地址		

Part I Listening and Speaking

Task 1 Listening Practice

Exercise 1

Directions: Now you will hear a short passage. Listen carefully and choose the best answer from the four choices.

1. Amazon.com was founded in _____.
   A. 1998　　　　　　　B. 1996　　　　　　　C. 1969
2. The Seattle-based company began selling _____.
   A. CDs online　　　　B. books online　　　C. videos online
3. You can find all the books of your favorite author by _____.
   A. sending an email　B. signing up online　C. clicking the mouse
4. In Internet shopping, payment is made _____.
   A. with a check　　　B. in cash　　　　　　C. by credit card

Exercise 2

Directions: Now you will hear a conversation. You are required to put in the missing information.

Clark: Do you know what is shopping online?
Ketty: Yes. I bought a lot of things from the ___1___.
Clark: Really? Could you tell me some ___2___ of it?
Ketty: Of course. Firstly, it is convenient. You can buy anything you want and they will ___3___ to your home or any place you want.
Clark: Woe, that is great..
Ketty: Yes. What's more, it is much cheaper than the goods in big shopping centers.
Clark: Ah, that is quite a ___4___ for shopping. What are the disadvantages?
Ketty: Well, the biggest problem is that you can't see the real goods; you can only look at the pictures ad some introduction of it. Besides, you cannot try them on if you want to buy some clothes or shoes, so sometimes the goods you buy may not fit you so well.
Clark: I see. What can I do if they don't fit?
Ketty: You can return them if you ___5___ with the goods.
Clark: In this case, shopping online is really convenient. Thanks for the introduction!
Ketty: My pleasure.

Exercise 3

Directions: Now you will hear a conversation. You are required to put in the missing information.

Danny: Aunt Cindy, do you shop online often?
Cindy: Yes. It's very ___1___ and the price is even lower.
Danny: Last week, I tried to buy some books online, but I didn't know how to pay for them.
Cindy: You should open an ___2___ at the online bank first. After that you can buy anything online.
Danny: Are there many things online?
Cindy: Sure. You can find everything ___3___. For example, this is a second-hand cellphone store.
Danny: What? Can you even buy cellphones online?
Cindy: Actually, you can do more than that: you can even sell your old cellphone here.
Danny: Really? How to do that?
Cindy: Take some pictures of your old cellphone, then upload them onto line with a ___4___ about it and leave your telephone number. If someone is interested in it, they will contact you.
Danny: That's amazing! I will try it some day.
Cindy: Shopping online is getting more and more popular. It's a real revolution about people's ___5___.

Exercise 4

Directions: Now you will hear a short passage. Listen carefully and decide whether the following statements are true or false.

_____ 1. Dangdang Inc. only sells books.
_____ 2. Dangdang Inc. Has been in e-commerce for less than 10 years.
_____ 3. You can buy electronic products with high quality on its website.
_____ 4. Compared with other e-commerce companies, Dangdang Inc. is not very large.
_____ 5. If you buy from Dangdang Inc., the goods can be delivered to your address.

Task 2 Oral Practice

Exercise 1

Directions: Suppose you're a buyer. You're going to buy something online. Follow the sample to make a conversation with your partner to discuss the purchase procedure.

A: Do you do a lot of shopping online?

B: Not really. I like surfing the Internet and see what's available, but I usually prefer to actually see and touch what I'm buying before I pay for it. Sometimes, I'll look at something in a shop, but later buy it online if it's cheaper. You don't like buying things online, do you?

A: Yes. I'm a little worried about security. You never know who's trying to find out your codes and passwords. Aren't you worry about that?

B: Not really. I know that it happens, but if you buy from reputable companies with secure websites, it should be OK.

A: Really? Can you recommend some reliable sellers or security measures?

B: Well, it's always recommended that you keep your credit cards and payment codes for yourself, and if possible, change your codes and passwords regularly. Always check for security when you are using a public computer.

A: Good idea! Have you ever had any unpleasant experience about shopping online?

B: Oh, yes, but only once. When the book I bought arrived, I found the book old and shabby, and several pages were even missing.

A: What did you do then?

B: I contacted the seller and made a complaint. Luckily, he admitted his mistake and exchanged one for me.

A: Is it complicated to exchange an unwanted item?

B: Not really. You just have to send it back, state your reasons and wait for the new one to arrive. Of course, it may take a few days.

Exercise 2

Directions: The following is the process of returning unwanted goods purchased online. Discuss with your partner or in group to describe the whole process in English.

Returns are easy

① Print label & authorisation.

② Prepare package.
(Include return authorisation)

③ Attach return label.

④ Send it!

Part II Reading

Text A

Before Reading:
1. Do you know what e-business is?
2. Compared with traditional business, what the advantages of e-business?

Introduction to E-business

E-business is the application of Internet technologies to business processes. However it is more than information technology tools or straight e-commerce. It also implies that the organization, especially its managers, are willing and receptive to radical changes that such new business techniques and tools bring. Its benefits come not just from the efficiencies and automation of a company's internal processes but from its ability to spread the efficiency gains to the business systems of its suppliers and customers.

An e-enterprise (participating in e-business) is defined as an enterprise prepared to conduct commerce in this new economy. This means it has created and embraced a business strategy informed by changing economics, new opportunities, and new threats. It has laid down the necessary technology infrastructure to support new business processes. Thus prepared, the enterprise is able to conduct e-commerce: the commercial exchange value (money, goods, services, or information) between an enterprise and an external entity over a universal electronic medium.

It is important to understand that e-commerce and e-business are more than just electronics and commerce/business added together. They represent an entirely new way of doing business. They are therefore far more about strategy and management than they are about technology. In order to appreciate the importance of e-business, it is important to see it from the perspective of the transactional aspects of e-business, those that represent the business between different players.

Therefore, e-business is taken as the extension of business on to the Internet; the re-engineering of business processes for digitizing of the transactions; the restructuring of the frameworks, both private and public to carry out the transactions seamlessly; and the development of the capacity in society and enterprise for this.

Large enterprises are taking a more considered approach to the implementation of e-business, since they no longer fear the loss of business to dot-com competitors; internationally, the highly publicized collapse of many of dot-coms has reduced the competitive threat from e-business. Increasingly, e-business is being regarded as a process that can make existing companies and governments more efficient in how they manage suppliers, customers and internal business processes.

New Words

application	/ˌæplɪˈkeɪʃ(ə)n/	n.	适用,应用,运用;申请,请求
imply	/ɪmˈplaɪ/	v.	暗示;意味;隐含;说明,表明
receptive	/rɪˈsɛptɪv/	adj.	善于接受的;能容纳的;有接受力的;感受的,感官的
radical	/ˈrædɪk(ə)l/	adj.	根本的,基本的;激进的;彻底的
automation	/ˌɔːtəˈmeɪʃ(ə)n/	n.	自动化(技术),自动操作
embrace	/ɪmˈbreɪs/	v.	包括;包含;接受;信奉
infrastructure	/ˈɪnfrəstrʌktʃə/	n.	基础设施;基础建设
represent	/ˌrɛprɪˈzɛnt/	v.	表现,象征;代表,代理;扮演;
perspective	/pəˈspɛktɪv/	n.	观点,看法;远景;景色;洞察力
extension	/ɪkˈstɛnʃ(ə)n/	n.	伸展,扩大;延长,延期
digitize	/ˈdɪdʒɪtaɪz/	v.	将资料数字化
framework	/ˈfreɪmwɜːk/	n.	构架;框架;(体系的)结构;机构,组织
seamless	/ˈsiːmləs/	adj.	无缝的;无漏洞的 (seamlessly: adv.)
approach	/əˈprəʊtʃ/	n.	方法;途径;接近
implementation	/ˌɪmplɪmɛnˈteɪʃ(ə)n/	n.	成就;贯彻;安装启用
dot-com			网络公司(仅在互联网上开展业务)
collapse	/kəˈlæps/	n.	垮台;(身体的)衰弱
competitive	/kəmˈpɛtɪtɪv/	adj.	竞争的,比赛的;(价格等)有竞争力的;(人)好竞争的

Phrases and Expressions

be defined as	被称为
lay down	规定
be regarded as	被视为

Exercises

I. Answer the following questions according to the passage.

1. What is the implication of e-business?

   _____

2. What preparations do enterprises make to enter into e-Business?

   _____

3. What is more important for successful e-Business, technology or management?

   _____

4. What should enterprises do to carry out successful e-Business?

   _____

5. What is the attitude of large enterprises to e-Business? Why?

   _____

II. Fill in the blanks with the proper words and expressions given below, changing the form if necessary.

imply	collapse	digitize	approach	competitive
embrace	create	radical	transaction	seamless

1. _____ sports encourage children to work together.
2. Not all the workers can _____ the technical reforms in the factory.
3. It was an incredibly _____ decision.
4. This company kept detailed records of all its major _____.
5. The novel shifts _____ from the present to the past.
6. Some old films _____ for better visual effects.
7. The U. S. auto industry almost _____ last year due to severe competition.
8. The salesman _____ that this type of cars were not good value for money.
9. Scientists now believed that the universe _____ by a big explosion.
10. The professor is trying a new _____ to teaching languages.

III. Translate the following sentences into Chinese.

1. The price of your products are not competitive in our market.
2. The first two years after graduation is radical to your career life.
3. We take it as an honor to be invited to your wedding party.
4. Are you implying that I am responsible for the accident?

IV. Translate the following sentences into English.

1. 政府正采取更谨慎的方法解决经济危机。
2. 茶被看作适合各类人群的健康饮料。
3. 运动可以被定义为连续的位置变化。
4. 出租车必须遵守警方制定的新规则。
5. 这本书是从一个小女孩的视角写的。

Text B

Before Reading:
1. Do you know what e-money is?
2. Can you list some forms of e-money?

E-Money

The increasing popularity of the Internet and e-commerce meant that it was necessary to find new ways of purchasing goods and services. Currently, there are three major electronic payment schemes available:

- Using credit card numbers
- Electronic checks
- Electronic money

The concept of e-money is simple: the users can simply transfer payments from their own bank accounts to the account of the merchant, electronically and securely over the Internet. E-money comes in two commercial forms: a plastic card with microchips called a smart card and in software form, called electronic cash. A smart card is about the size of a credit card. It is a plastic card into which a microprocessor chip is embedded. Smart cards are used to store money value, which can also be used to purchase goods or services over the Internet. To use a smart card, a special device called a smart card reader is needed.

E-money is of two types: identified e-money and anonymous e-money. Identified e-money contains information revealing the identity of the individual who originally withdrew the e-money from the bank. A transaction path of the e-money can also be created, which means that the bank can keep track of the movements of the e-money through the e-market.

In the case of anonymous e-money, once the e-money is withdrawn from the bank, the identity of the person who uses the money will remain unknown and the bank cannot track the movement of the e-money through the market.

E-money is created electronically, however counterfeiting and double spending are still possible. There are different e-money systems that can be used to detect or prevent double spending, such as the online e-money system.

An online e-money system requires the merchant to contact the bank's computer containing a database of all the e-money spent at the point of sale. This will enable the merchant to verify if the customer's e-money is still valid or usable. In this way, the merchant can either accept or refuse a transaction.

E-money has the following benefits:

• Reduces company expenses. Transferring digital money over the Internet is much cheaper than using conventional banking systems, since there is no need to use extra forms or hire tellers.

• Makes transaction procedures easy. There is no need to fill out forms or make telephone inquiries to the bank.

• Promotes fast transaction. There is real-time coordination of information and the transaction without the needs for intermediary services.

• Secured payments. E-money banks also use SET-enabled servers and SSL-enhanced browsers providing more secure electronic payment.

New Words

scheme	/ski:m/	n.	计划;体系;阴谋
microchip	/ˈmʌɪkrə(ʊ)tʃɪp/	n.	微晶片;微型集成电路片
microprocessor	/ˌmʌɪkrə(ʊ)ˈprəʊsɛsə/	n.	微处理器
embed	/ɪmˈbɛd/	v.	把……嵌入;栽种;
anonymous	/əˈnɒnɪməs/	adj.	无名的;假名的;匿名的
reveal	/rɪˈviːl/	v.	显露;揭露;泄露
counterfeit	/ˈkaʊntəfɪt/	v.	仿制,造假;假装,伪装
verify	/ˈvɛrɪfʌɪ/	v.	核实;证明;判定
valid	/ˈvalɪd/	adj.	有效的;有法律效力的
coordination	/kəʊˌɔːdɪˈneɪʃ(ə)n/	n.	协作;配合
intermediary	/ˌɪntəˈmiːdɪəri/	adj.	中间的;媒介的;中途的

Phrases and Expressions

keep track of	记录;与……保持联系
fill out	填写(表格)

Proper Names

SSL	Netscape公司于1996年推出的安全协议,其主要目的是为网络环境中两个通信应用进程之间提供一个安全通道。

Exercises

I. Read the above passage carefully and decide whether the following statements are true or false.

　　____ 1. Traditional payment methods still work for e-commerce so there is no need for new ways.
　　____ 2. The online e-money system is used to protect the customers.
　　____ 3. All smart cards contain microprocessor chips.
　　____ 4. Companies have to spend extra money on digital money transference.
　　____ 5. It is easy and also secure to use e-money.

II. Fill in the blanks with the proper words and expressions given below, changing the form if necessary.

| embed | coordinate | reveal | track | microchip |
| verify | valid | purchase | detect | tradition |

1. They appointed a new manager to _____ the work of the team. .
2. People began _____ their scientific theory by doing experiments.
3. For foreign holidays you will need a _____ passport.
4. She refused to _____ the secrets of her daughter.
5. You become so deeply absorbed in an activity that you lose _____ of time.
6. The young couple _____ their picture in the glass.
7. Their instruments can _____ the slightest change in temperature.
8. He _____ a ticket and went up on the top deck.
9. The tiger was tagged with a _____ to enable its movements to be tracked.
10. Spring Festival is a _____ Chinese holiday for family reunion.

III. Pay attention to different parts of speech and select the appropriate word to fill in the blank.

1. detect, detective, detection, detector
　　a. A metal _____ is installed in the entrance of the theatre.
　　b. This writer is famous for his _____ stories.
　　c. Many forms of cancer can be cured if _____ early.
　　d. The plane flew very low to avoid _____ by radar.
2. identify, identity, identical, identification
　　a. My work hours are almost _____ with my daughter's school hours.
　　b. Can you _____ the person who robbed you?
　　c. The bodies were sent to the hospital for _____.
　　d. We still don't know the _____ of the other man in the picture.

• Unit 8   E-commerce •

3. popular, popularity, popularize, popularly
   a. It is _____ known that too much exercise can do harm to the body.
   b. Hilary is the most _____ girl at school.
   c. It is a challenging work to _____ some scientific theories.
   d. The _____ of smart phones has grown dramatically in the last five years.
4. serve, service, servant
   a. I am and remain a faithful _____ of my country.
   b. My father _____ as the chief engineer in this company.
   c. The _____ in that hotel was terrible and I would never return.
5. tradition, traditional, traditionally
   a. Having dinner together on New Year's Eve is an important _____ in my family.
   b. Married women have _____ been treated as dependent on their husbands.
   c. A _____ organization or person prefers older methods and ideas to modern ones.

IV. Class Work

   The whole class is divided into two groups. One group is required to list the advantages and disadvantages of e-money and its transaction, and the other is required to list the advantages and disadvantages of traditional money and transaction. Then a debate will be organized for each group to argue for their opinion.

Part III Writing

Orders

订单(订货信)是请求卖方供应具体数量的商品,其形式可以是信件,也可以采用印制的订货单。

Example (范例):

I. An example of the order form

ORDER FORM

7th November, 2012

China National Imp.& Exp. Corp.
SHANGHAI, China

Qnty	Item	Catalogue No.	CIF Sydney NET
200	Bed Sheets, 160cm, blue	67	$ 2.50 each
200	Bed Sheets, 120cm, primrose	89	3.00 each
300	Pillow Cases, blue	101	1.80 a pair
500	Pillow Cases, primrose	120	1.80 a pair

Packing: In cotton cloth bales.
Shipment: Prompt shipment from Shanghai.
Payment: By irrevocable L/C available by draft at sight.

II. An example of the order letter

18th June, 2013

China National Import & Export Corp.
SHANGHAI, China

Dear Sirs,

Thank you for your letter of 12th June sending us patterns of cotton prints. We find both quality and prices satisfactory and are pleased to give you an order for the following items on the understanding that they will be supplied from current stock at the prices named:

Quantity	Pattern No.	Prices (net)
300 yards	72	33p per yard
450 yards	82	38p per yard
300 yards	84	44p per yard
		CIF Lagos

We expect to find a good market for these cottons and hope to place further and larger orders with you in the near future.

• Unit 8   E-commerce •

> Our usual terms of payment are cash against documents and we hope they will be acceptable to you.
>
> Please send us your confirmation of sales in duplicate.
>
> Yours faithfully
Crombongo Textiles Co., Ltd.
Manager

Tips (写作注意事项)

The essential qualities of an order are accuracy and clarity. An order or an order letter should:

a) include full details of description, quantities and prices and quote article numbers, if any;

b) state mode of packing, port of destination and time of shipment;

c) confirm the terms of payment as agreed upon in previous negotiations.

Sometimes, buyers will seek to protect themselves by making their order subject to certain penalties should the the contracted terms not be fulfilled.

However, according to the commercial law, the buyer's order is an offer to buy and the arrangement is not legally binding until the seller has accepted the offer. After that, both parties are legally bound to honor their agreement.

Useful Expression in an order letter

1. We enclose a trial order. If the quality is up to our expectation, we shall send further orders in the near future.

2. If this first order is satisfactorily executed, we shall place further orders with you.

3. The material supplied must be absolutely waterproof, and we place our order subject to this guarantee.

4. All these items are urgently required by our customers. We therefore, hope you will make delivery at an early date.

5. We enclose our order, but must point out that the falling market here will leave us little or no margin of profit. We must ask you for a better price in respect of future supplies.

6. We are expecting a good market for these shoes, hoping to place further orders in large quantity, and your prompt attention to this order will be appreciated.

Exercise:

Directions: This part is to test your ability to do practical writing. You are required to complete the following payment reminder with the help of Chinese equivalent. Remember not to translate the Chinese word for word.

17th July, 2013

H. Simpson & Co. Ltd
298 South Street
SYDNEY, Australia

Dear sirs,

　　We thank you for your letter of 2nd July and are glad to _____ (告诉您，我们对您的样品很满意).

　　_____ (随信附上我们的首次订单). We hope the following items will be supplied from stock at the price named:

"Peony" Raincoats

Quantity	Pattern No.	Unit Prices
100 men's (M)	23	USD 13.00
100 men's (S)	24	USD 12.50
100 women's (M)	35	USD 12.50
100 women's (S)	36	USD 12.00

　　We believe _____ (如果质量好，该品牌的雨衣会在我方市场畅销) and we hope to _____ (很快能大量订货).

　　Your prompt attention to this order will be appreciated.

　　　　　　　　　　　　　　　　　　　　　　　　Yours Sincerely
　　　　　　　　　　　　　　　　　　　　　　Brown, Clarke & Company
　　　　　　　　　　　　　　　　　　　　　　　　Sales Manager

Part IV Cultural Express

Internet Marketing

At its core, the mission of marketing is to attract and retain customers. To accomplish this goal, a traditional bricks-and-mortar marketer uses a variety of marketing variables — including pricing, advertising, and channel choice — to satisfy current and new customers.

With the emergence of the Internet and its associated technology enable screen-to-face interfaces (e.g. mobile phones, interactive television), a new era of marketing has emerged. If traditional marketing is about creating exchanges that simultaneously satisfy the firm and customers, then Internet marketing is the process of building and maintaining customer relationships through online activities to facilitate the exchange of ideas, products, and services that satisfy the goals of both parties.

Like a traditional-marketing program, an Internet-marketing program involves a process. The seven stages of the Internet-marketing program process are setting corporate and business-unit strategy, framing the market opportunity, formulating the marketing strategy, designing the customer experience, designing the marketing program, crafting the customer interface, and evaluating the results of the marketing program. These seven stages must be coordinated and internally consistent. While the process can be described in a simple linear fashion, the marketing strategist often has to loop back and forth during the seven stages.

The goal of marketing is to build and create lasting customer relationship. Hence, the focal point shifts from finding customers to nurturing a sufficient number of committed, loyal customers. Successful marketing programs move target customers through three stages of relationship building: awareness, exploration, and commitment. It is important to stress that the goal of Internet marketing is not simply building relationships with online customers. Rather, the goal is to build offline as well as online relationships. The Internet marketing program may well be part of a broader campaign to satisfy customers who use both online and offline services.

By definition, Internet marketing deals with levers that are available in the world of the Internet. However, as noted above, the success of an Internet marketing program may rest with traditional, offline marketing vehicles. Consider, for example, the recruiting and job-seeking service Monster.com. Monster's success can be tied directly to the effectiveness of its television advertising and, in particular, its widely successful Super Bowl ads of the past two years.

At the core of both online and offline marketing program is the concept of exchange. In both the online and offline worlds, exchange is still the heart of marketing. In the new economy, firms must by very sensitive to cross-channel exchanges. That is, an online marketing program must be evaluated according to its overall exchanges in retail stores. Firms must be increasingly sensitive to these cross-channel effects if they are to measure the independent effects of online and offline marketing programs.

Supplementary Vocabulary

Authentication and Accredit	认证和授权
B2B: B to B (Business to Business)	企业间的电子交易
B2C: B to C (Business to Consumer)	电子零售,企业对消费者的交易
Commercial Software	商业软件
Commercial Online Service	商业在线服务
Cyber economy	网络经济
Digital Certificate	数字凭证
Digital Cash	数字现金
Electronic Mall	电子购物中心
EDI (Electronic Data Interchange)	电子数据交换
Electronic Funds Transfer	电子资金转帐(EFT)
Encrypt and decrypt a message	对信息加密和解密
E-tailware	电子零售软件
E-Traditional Industry	传统产业的电子化
E-wallet	电子钱包
Interactive Television	互动式电视
ISP (Internet Serve Provider)	网络服务供应商
Payment activation code	支付激活码
Personal Marketing	个性化营销
Promotion On Internet	网上促销
Reseller Online	网上中间商
Virtual Electronic Commerce City	电子商城